BLUE RIDGE PARKWAY GUIDE

Grandfather Mountain to
Great Smoky Mountains National Park

**Grandfather Mountain to
Great Smoky Mountains
National Park
291.9–469 miles**

Blue Ridge Parkway Guide

by William G. Lord

Menasha Ridge Press

Text copyright © William G. Lord, 1981
First Menasha Edition, Seventh Printing, 2000

Menasha Ridge Press
P. O. Box 43673
Birmingham, AL 35243
www.menasharidge.com

Distributed by The Globe Pequot Press

Library of Congress Cataloging–in–Publication Data

Lord, William George, 1921–

    Blue Ridge Parkway Guide : Grandfather Mountain
    to Great Smoky Mountain National Park 291.9 to
    469 miles
    by William G. Lord

    p. cm.

    Rev. ed. of: The Blue Ridge Guide. 1959–1963
    Includes bibliographical references.

    ISBN 0–89732–119–7

    1. Automobile Travel—Blue Ridge Parkway
    (NC and VA)—Guidebooks.

    2. Blue Ridge Parkway (NC and VA)—Guidebooks.

I. Title
GV1024.L58   1992

917.55—dc20   92-28238   CIP

The author thanks the following for their assistance: Superintendent Gary Everhardt, Resident Landscape Architect Bob Hope, Historian Dr. Harley E. Jolley, and Interpreter Hoyt C. Roth, all of the Blue Ridge Parkway; Superintendent J. Moyer, U.S. Postal Service, Charlottesville, Va.; John H. Reeves, Jr., Virginia Military Institute, Lexington, Va.; Virginia State Extension Specialist W. A. McElfresh, Blacksburg, Va.; Hugh Morton, Grandfather Mountain, Linville, N.C.; Prof. Lewis E. Anderson, Department of Botany, Duke University, Durham, N.C.; Alice Carol Tuckwiller, Roanoke Public Library, Roanoke, Va.; Odell Little, Jefferson, N.C.; Office of the Mayor, Galax, Va.; Bea Simpson, Community Action Programs, Galax, Va.; Mary H. Esser, Public Information Specialist, U.S. Forest Service, Asheville, N.C.; and E. F. Striplin, Jr., Norfolk and Western Railway, Roanoke, Va. Special thanks are due Agnes M. Elton, Pittsburgh, Pa. for manuscript preparation and Dr. Cratus Williams, Appalachian State University, Boone, N.C. for review of folk language.

Blue Ridge farm

Blue Ridge Parkway

The Blue Ridge Parkway idea probably originated in the mind of a motorist years ago, traveling over a bumpy mountain road. "How nice it would be," he mused aloud, "if there were a smooth, easy way over the mountains and we could lazy-along and enjoy the view."

The idea found a place in the minds of many men, but for years it had to wait. Building a road through the mountains is a giant task.

Now the Parkway is a reality. It happened something like this. On a pleasant summer day in August 1933, President Franklin Delano Roosevelt came to Shenandoah National Park, Va., on an inspection tour of the Civilian Conservation Corps. Among his most enjoyable miles were those viewing scenery on Shenandoah's Skyline Drive.

Virginia's Senator Harry F. Byrd, a member of the presidential party, suggested the grandiloquent project of constructing a road over the mountain crests connecting Shenandoah and Great Smoky Mountains National Parks. President Roosevelt gave his enthusiastic approval and the idea moved toward reality.

The Administration placed the project under the joint authority of the National Park Service and the Bureau of Public Roads. Virginia and North Carolina contributed to the venture by purchasing land for the motor road right-of-way, and on June 30, 1936, the Seventy-fourth Congress passed the act giving legal status to the Blue Ridge Parkway.

When news reached Aunt Caroline Brinegar, a-sittin' and a-rockin' in her cabin high in the Blue Ridge by Air Bellows Gap, she slapped her knee and laughed at such "an onheered of notion. One of them hard surface roads like they have below the mountains? Why, Lord have mercy, no body a-livin' could put one of them through here."

Still, Aunt Caroline was mighty interested. Every Sunday she'd pause from a-trompin' the treadles of her four-poster loom and hurry across the hollow to Mrs. Krause's and have her read the weekly news. The many articles about Parkway plans and progress soon had her believing "they just might build a road."

Then one day she heard dogs a-barkin', and looking out from the porch stoop she saw surveyors with their chains and rods. Then she knew the road was a-comin' fur sure.

The Parkway is a way of travel through the Southern Highlands dedicated to the recreation motorist. In a manner of thinking it expresses the cooperation of the engineer and landscape architect. The engineer solved and smoothed the obstacles of a seemingly impassable terrain. The landscape architect healed the road scars with green and designed parking overlooks and recreation areas for leisurely enjoyment. Log cabin exhibits along the way preserve the tang of old-timey days.

Recreation areas, varying in size from several hundred to several thousand acres, are wilderness gems for those who enjoy the out-of-doors. Development for visitor use includes picnic grounds, camp and trailer sites, rest rooms, water fountains, and hiking trails.

Service stations, lodging, eating facilities, and handicraft shops operated by concessionaires are at intervals along the way. Nearby are varied resort facilities generally indicated by standard Parkway signs.

The Parkway extends 469 miles from its Shenandoah National Park terminus at Rockfish Gap, Va., to the Great Smoky Mountains National Park at Cherokee, North Carolina. Every mile is maintained and protected by the Parkway staff.

Rangers meet with Parkway neighbors and arrange the leasing of government land that is suitable for pature and crops. The farm scene is thereby brought to the roadside and the 800-foot strip of Parkway flows along in harmony with the native landscape. The Parkway also extends through long stretches of National Forests, guardians of our timber and water sources.

The park ranger force, manned by men and women in forest green uniforms and broad-brimmed hats, patrols the motor road to serve the Parkway visitor and protect the area.

Park naturalists, by means of exhibits, living history demonstrations, nature trails, and illustrated lectures, interpret the storied highlands and make a visit more meaningful and enjoyable.

Headquarters are in Asheville, N.C. The Blue Ridge Parkway, a unit of the National Park System, welcomes your visit. The Parkway is yours to enjoy and protect.

Mountain Ranges Along the Blue Ridge Parkway
Most of the Parkway's 469 miles roll atop 355 miles of the Blue Ridge. The remaining distance is through the heart of the Southern Highlands over the Black Mountains, the Great Craggies, Pisgah Ledge, and the Great Balsams. The last group intersects still another range, the Plott Balsams, extending on either side of the Parkway like the wings of a great eagle.

The Blue Ridge, stretching from Pennsylvania to Georgia, forms the eastern rampart of the central and southern Appalachians. The Appalachians comprise the great eastern mountain system extending from Canada to Alabama.

The Parkway commences its journey at Rockfish Gap, rolling southwest from Shenandoah National Park. For over a hundred miles en route to Roanoke, Va., the mountains form a massive barrier rising between the piedmont foothills on the east, and the Great Valley on the west. Beyond the valley loom the Alleghenies. Midway to Roanoke the mountains are severed by the seven-mile gorge of the mighty James, flowing from the Alleghenies to the Atlantic. At this point, mile 65, the Parkway dips to its lowest elevation, 650 feet. It soon weaves up to the crest line again, and on Apple Orchard Mountain attains its highest elevation in Virginia, 3,950 feet above the sea.

From Apple Orchard the Parkway gradually descends through a deep green forest of hemlock and hardwoods onto a long finger of the

Blue Ridge pointing into the Roanoke basin. Again the view commands the horizon, east and west. The city of Roanoke, within the basin, lies surrounded by the Blue Ridge and the Alleghenies.

Between miles 102-132, the Parkway cruises below the western slopes of the Blue Ridge, across the Roanoke River Valley. The Roanoke flows leisurely from the nearby Alleghenies through a broad break in the mountain wall. In this vicinity the Blue Ridge is actually a discontinuous series of free-standing elevations.

South of the Roanoke lies the Blue Ridge plateau, a long uplands wedged between the piedmont and the Great Valley. Here the Blue Ridge forms the eastern rim of the plateau—a ridge in name only.

The Parkway travels close by the rim, with a view of rolling mountain farmland and frequent vistas of the misty piedmont. At mile 216.9 the Parkway and the Blue Ridge move into North Carolina, 252 miles from Great Smoky Mountains National Park.

The Carolina portion of the plateau builds up from a rolling uplands to a surging array of humpbacked mountains and swooping valleys. At Ridge Junction, mile 355, the unruly terrain runs into the massive sides of the Black Mountains, while the Blue Ridge swings southeast on its way to Georgia.

The Parkway skirts the southern edge of the short, ponderous Blacks through a virgin forest of spruce and balsam—and into the heartland of the highlands.

From the adjoining Great Craggies, with their weird forest of wind-stunted trees, the Parkway enters the Asheville area and the French Broad River Valley. As in the Roanoke region, the Blue Ridge lies eastward. But here the river finds no passage to the ocean and so flows over the long inland route to the Mississippi.

Pisgah Ledge carries the Parkway from Asheville southwest to Tanasee Bald. Scenery is breathtaking over the entire Parkway, but from Pisgah Ledge it portrays the meaning of spectacular.

From Tanasee Bald the Parkway swings northwest along the Great Balsams. Like the Blacks, they form one of several transverse ranges at right angles to the northeast southwest trend of the Appalachians.

At Richland Balsam, mile 431, the Parkway attains its maximum elevation of 6,053 feet.

En route to the Great Smokies, the Parkway bisects the Plott Balsams and then gradually descends through the land of the Cherokee. Here is journey's end or beginning, whichever way you take it.

Through the Seasons along the Parkway
Spring is a time gay with blossoms and bird song. The climate is brisk, the mood vibrant. The horned lark breaks into melody in March, when the maple tints the leafless forest with red.

But the Parkway is still too much under winter's spell and not up to its best company manners. The wind is often rough. Snow and ice have sudden ways.

Along comes April and the serviceberry tosses its white blossoms like a bunch of suspended snowflakes. The ground is dappled with the white flowers of great chickweed, early saxifrage, blood-root, and stonecrop. And many meadows seem to be yellow seas of field cress.

Perhaps you'll see mountain folk out gathering shoots of cress and other "sallet greens."

The birds are in jubilant tune—field sparrow, towhee, Carolina junco, brown thrasher, and meadowlark. The roadside has a sudden abundance of groundhogs and rabbits, eagerly stuffing themselves with new green food. Skunks nose in the turf, totally unaware of anything but their appetites.

The weather is still cool, but the sun is bolder. Many days bring that lazy, indolent feeling—spring fever.

With May, spring comes into its own. Dogwood lays a milky way beneath the leafing forest. Oak leaves are the size of a squirrel's ear—cue for the mountain man to plant his corn.

Wood warblers are passing through, pausing in almost every tree to sing and hunt for food. Many of them, knowing the mountains to be cool as the northern forests, will remain and nest.

Warblers are the big event of spring migration. A good day's birding will note a score or more. Pause at almost any recreation area, and the telltale songs will identify the ovenbird, the chestnut-sided, the black-and-white, the black-throated blue, the prairie, and the hooded warblers. In mid-May the cuckoos, both black-billed and yellow-billed, have arrived, and spring migration is about complete.

The spring flood of flowers has broken in full splendor. Azaleas trim the roadside and brighten the forest edge with pink and flame. Fraser magnolia unpeels its large creamy flowers, like sequins among the leaves. The yellow poplar "lights up" with blooms of candle-glow yellow. Locust and cherry join in with pink and white.

Somewhere in May a cold snap drops in. Usually it occurs when the blackberry thickets cast a "snow" of blossoms over old pastures and fence rows. This is the mountaineer's "blackberry winter."

But spring bounds back and rollicks into June with the bloom high tide culminating in a splendor of azalea, catawba rho-dodendron, and mountain laurel.

The birds are busy rearing their first hatch. Grouse and wild turkey guide their obedient broods through the shrub cover of the forest's edge, imparting an inborn knack of survival. It has been said that young birds deprived of parental training through some accident to the devoted hens are less capable than those brought up "right and proper." They fall easy prey to the fox, the wildcat, and the hunter.

In the remote regions of the Parkway another devoted parent set, the ravens, guide their raucous, intelligent young'uns from crag to crag. Unlike the more abundant crows, they do not gather in flocks but live in family groups.

The pregnant doe retires to a thicket and quietly gives birth to her spotted fawn. Silence is an inborn virtue that protects parent and offspring. When the fawn is left alone, it lies mute as a sun-dappled shadow until the doe noiselessly returns.

Spring seems to end when the mountain laurel fades and summer comes in with elder bloom and the "hot weather" song of the indigo bunting. Mountain summer is sunny, but cooler than in the humid lowlands.

In the evening a coolness drifts over the land. Taking a stroll at dusk, one doesn't mind putting on a sweater to listen to the whip-poorwill and to see large moths flutter in the twilight.

During summer, showers come often but seldom last more than an hour—rarely enough to interfere with an outing. Now and then the days grow damp and gray with fog. Mountain fog closes in like a mystery, and even the short trails looping from the parking overlooks seem like adventure in another world.

Most days by far are golden. The summer scene is one of green forests, green meadows, roadside flowers, and trim fields of corn, cabbage, oats, and buckwheat.

The forest has miles of dark rhododendron growing like still another forest beneath it. As you know, the catawba has bloomed, but July is the time for the rosebay. Its shell-pink blossoms convey a peppermint coolness in the leather-slick leaves.

Midsummer bees are feasting in the sourwood trees. The leaves are literally crowned with whisk-like groups of white, urn-shaped flowers laden with nectar that bees make into a honey so sweet and refined it will not turn to sugar. The summer's harvest will soon be ready to pour over hot buttered biscuits and toast.

Most of the roadside flowers through July are familiar in fields throughout the East—wild carrot, daisy, and black-eyed Susan.

Where the woods are moist, tall black snakeroot stretches up, bearing a fuzzy white "spike" of blossoms often referred to as a "fairy candle." In like places the ferns abound—the tall cinnamon, the dark green Christmas fern, and the lacy lady fern. In the high, cool forests of the Blacks, Craggies, and Balsams grows the American shield fern, the most luxuriant of them all. Its filmy haunt is also the home of the veery, "the thrush that sings like a shadow."

The forest borders through this alpine niche are trimmed with lilies, coneflower, and Oswego tea.

Late summer has its colorful time along moist meadows where boneset, ironweed, and Joe-pye weed weave a design of white, purple, and lavender-pink.

Crops are ripening. Corn is at full tassel and stacks of oats are arrayed on fields of golden stubble. Buckwheat is white and sweet scented, but not for long. A hint of brown shows seeds are beginning to form.

There's no bird song, unless you'll accept the woodpecker's drum. Well, they've had a busy time—courting, nest-building, and family-raising. Now they go about their way quietly.

The goldfinch is one joyous exception. August finds him in exuberant voice and with plenty to sing about. He postponed his courting until the thistle bloomed and provided "thistle down" for nest building. Now his young are newly hatched and cozy.

Autumn has a subtle manner. The forest seems typically green.

But look; a dogwood turned red brings sudden awareness that summer is taking leave.

The dogwood is apparently not alone. There are others now that meet the eye. Gum and sourwood have turned, all giving a dapple of red to the green. Here and there a maple flares like a pastel torch.

But once noticed, fall does not turn rapidly into its hardwood colorama. There is plenty of time for aster and goldenrod, patterns of white, blue, and yellow stippling the woods and fields.

Far overhead the sky is a limitless arena for the hawks migrating southward along the mountain crests. It takes a keen eye to catch them. Traveling solo or in scattered flocks, the hawks drift into a fast rising thermal column of warm air and spiral upward in tight turns until they are often lost from view. Reaching the top of the lift they break off in a glide that may be miles long.

Meanwhile, fall color is building up. The green mountains become mottled with yellow and red as the bright tones seep into the leaves. Those who have seen it sense the expectancy.

With flamboyant suddenness, a crescendo of color glows brief and brilliant over the highlands—improvisation of red, purple, orange, and yellow by maple, hickory, birch, and oak against the deep green of pine and hemlock. The peak will last about three days and then slowly fall prey to brownness and the wind.

The sharp tang of autumn perks up the buck deer. A shy recluse during summer, he bounds across the motor road with white-tail flag held high.

Squirrels nimble-foot through the oaks snipping the acorns and then scurrying down to bury them for winter. Possums in a much more leisurely manner feed on the frost-ripened fruit of the persimmon tree. The black bear fills his enormous paunch with a harvest of acorns, persimmons, beechnuts, and stolen honey.

Winter chases autumn away with windy buffets. The trees are bare, the fields are brown. Life puts out a holding force of crows and juncos, then retires until spring.

The Mountain Indians

During the 1730s, as the early settlers moved into the southern highlands of Virginia, they found a green, game-rich vastness, thriving with life but for one strange exception. No Indians. Abandoned campsites and corn fields indicated recent habitation, but now the Great Valley between the Alleghenies and the Blue Ridge stretched like a vast, uninhabited prairie. The mountain forests contained more bears than it did human beings. Occasionally hunting or war parties from distant tribes passed through, but where were the native red men?

John Lederer, an explorer commissioned by governor Sir William Berkeley of Virginia, crossed the Blue Ridge in 1669 and visited a village of the native Totero (or Tutelo) near the present site of Roanoke. He learned that they lived in constant dread of Iroquois warriors from New York and Canada. Few tribes could stand the skill and ferocity of the "Red Romans." The Totero and their Saponi kinsmen to the north were reduced to a remnant by the time the settlers arrived. It is also probable that whiskey and smallpox epidemics quickened their destruction.

For a few years a group of Totero and Saponi survivors lived in the Blue Ridge foothills south of Roanoke. In 1740 they moved to Canada and accepted the protection of their Iroquois conquerors. A cholera outbreak, tolled mournfully during the final month of sickness by a Mohawk chapel bell, ended their existence in 1800.

The Tuscarora Indians also lived a while in the eastern foothills of the Virginia Blue Ridge. A southern branch of the powerful Iroquois, they formerly lived on the Carolina coast in close proximity to white settlements. In the inevitable conflict, the Tuscaroras were defeated in a savage war, 1711-1713, and forced to leave.

During a gradual withdrawal to join their northern kinsmen, they tarried for a number of years below the mountains and frequently crossed paths with early settlers and hunters.

Another well-known tribe lived east of the Carolina Blue Ridge along the banks of the Catawba River that bears their name. According to tribal tradition, they came as buffalo hunters from the northwest. After a desperate struggle with the Cherokee, who claimed the territory, they succeeded in establishing themselves. Their language indicates a close relationship to the mighty Sioux of the western prairies.

The Catawba once totaled an estimated 5,000, but by 1721 the figure decreased to 1,200. Throughout most of their history they were friendly to the whites and often served as scouts against the Cherokee and other hostile tribes. A few hundred live today on a reservation by Sugar Creek, South Carolina.

Various other tribes lived in the Blue Ridge region of Virginia and Carolina, fading from history before the close of the eighteenth century. Among these were the Yeatkin, and the Saura (also known as Cheraw, and Sara) who gave their name to Sauratown Mountain, seen from Pilot Mountain Overlook, mile 189.3.

The Shawnee, inveterate foes of the Cherokee, are well known as the "Terrors of the Ohio Frontier." A number of their villages were formerly located in the Carolinas and Georgia. Presumably they were expelled by the Cherokee and, thereafter, often came from Ohio on vengeance raids.

The greatest Indian nation known to the white settlers of the Southern Highlands was the Cherokee. Throughout the genesis of our country they sought by force, statesmanship, and prayer to maintain a freedom of their own.

When the pioneers pushed onto the Cherokee lands in the 1770s, the Indians had withdrawn behind a mountain redoubt in the Great Balsam and Great Smoky region, resolved to retreat no further.

Despite a series of devastating wars and epidemics, the Cherokee showed remarkable recovery during each interval of peace. Prior to 1838 when the majority were forcibly expelled to reservations in the West, their numbers had swelled to twenty thousand. A few hundred who managed to hide out in the mountains were subsequently allowed to remain. Their descendants comprise the Eastern Band of Cherokees, successfully managing their affairs on the Qualla Reservation in the Great Smokies.

The Indian has been characterized as a fierce marauder constantly on the war path. Actually his inclinations were at least as peaceful as those of the white man and much of his warfare was a matter not of choice but of desperation.

The wiser of the red men knew the futility of opposing the on-pressing settlers, and attempted to preserve their land by diplomacy and negotiation. By far the most successful in this endeavor was Little Carpenter, or Attakulakula, of the Cherokee. A diminutive man, he, nonetheless, stood tall in the saddle and tall on oratory. His eloquence often calmed the hothead element and persuaded agreements between his people and the settlers.

Our ancestors, however, generally considered the Indian as an obstacle to be overcome like the wild beasts and the uncleared land. A promise to an Indian was not a promise, but merely a means to an end. Given the choice of extermination without a struggle, or fighting, the Indians chose to fight.

To a fatal degree, the red man was his own worst enemy. Instead of making a concerted effort against a common foe, each tribe pursued age-old hostilities against one another. While fighting the frontiersmen, the Cherokee were in a state of war with the Iroquois, Catawba, Shawnee, and Creek. The Catawba, though generally at peace with the settlers, lost many of their braves fighting the white man's battle against Iroquois, Shawnee, Cherokee, and Tuscarora.

In the Southern Highlands the Indians made two major efforts to throw back their uncompromising foes. The leaders of the first outbreak were the Shawnee, allies of the French, during the French and Indian War, 1754-1763. Stealthy guerrilla bands burned and massacred isolated homesteads along much of the Parkway region. A strange inertia gripped the frontier, born of panic and indifference. The defeat of the French gave the frontiersmen a chance to reassert themselves and in 1774 they marched into West Virginia and defeated the Indians at the Battle of Point Pleasant.

The Cherokee made the most protracted stand against the white men. Early in the 1700s they allied themselves with the British, and during the French and Indian War fought as allies with the American frontiersmen. The alliance with the "long-knives," as the frontiersmen were known to the Indians, was not destined to last. Largely of Scotch-Irish stock and far from friendly to the English king, the frontiersmen did not welcome the Cherokee as allies. The two tolerated each other until the end of the war and then faced off in a fight to the finish.

The Indians fought an effective guerrilla action of sniping and ambush, but could not match their foes in pitched combat. Each time violence burst forth, the whites organized under their leaders and drove into the mountain heartland of the Cherokee in North

Carolina, Tennessee, and Georgia, razing crops and villages. The starving survivors were forced to sue for peace.

Not all relations between the two races were hostile, however. For many years after contact was made with the mountain tribes about 1670, a flourishing fur trade existed. The Indians learned many advantages of the white man's way from traders who lived among them. The oncoming settlers profited from the Indian's knowledge of woodcraft and farming.

But, inevitably, the white man represented disaster to the Indians. His diseases, whiskey, and bullets, plus the land-hungry surge of the frontier, swept the red men to certain defeat.

Names Uncle Newt Calls 'Em

Our Parkway story grew from many sources such as libraries and courthouse records. But much came from a friendly, ever helpful group of mountain folk along the Parkway. These good neighbors are the honorary historians of their community. "You just go see Uncle Newt. He kin tell you 'most anything they is to know about."

From these many conversations Uncle Newt was born, a make-believe yet very real mountain man who "draps in" every few pages with his seasoned brand of mountain lore.

Uncle Newt is neither young nor old; he's just sort of today-like. He has a boy in the Army, and one daughter a-courtin', and two young'uns fur helpin' out about the farm.

The family—wife, man, and offspring—raise their own eggs and meat, do a heap of cannin' from the garden, and make most of their cash crop from burley, cabbages, apples, and sellin' a few Herefords each fall.

Uncle Newt is right proud of his most recent possession, a quarter-ton pickup, so new "hit still don't smell of the barnyard."

To avoid any misunderstanding: many of our local contacts had college degrees, spoke perfect English, and, like Uncle Newt, were gracious and helpful. Uncle Newt was born out of love and admiration for the mountaineer local color he represents.

With Uncle Newt's assistance, we'll endeavor to describe the geographic terms of the Southern Highlands.

Bald A high mountain that has (or had at the time it was named) a treeless area on or near its summit. The treeless patch may be barren or covered with grass or shrubs. Many of these fields are believed to have been caused by fires, repeatedly set by the Indians for game clearings. They are gradually returning to forest, some more rapidly than others, depending on the climate. Craggy Gardens, mile 364.

Bluffs "A big ole mountain that dips off sharp down one side." The Bluffs of Doughton Park, mile 241.

Butt "Ever had someone say he'd like to kick you in the pants? Well this here butt has a callin' likeness." Our map makers tend to change certain of the original names they consider too "salty." Craggy Pinnacle, mile 364.4, was once known as Buckner's Butt.

Cliff "A big ole rocky ridge and plenty steep. Most folks calls'm 'clifts.' " A rare term. Cedar Cliffs of Doughton Park, mile 241.

Dome A round-topped mountain, like a knob, but one of great stature. Craggy Dome, mile 364.1.

Peak A prominent, steep mountain, such as Clingman's Peak, seen at mile 349.9.

Piedmont The foothill country between the Blue Ridge and the Atlantic Coastal Plain.

Pinnacle A sharp, conical mountain. Craggy Pinnacle, seen at mile 364.4.

Range   A group of mountains defined by surrounding lowlands and forming a major drainage divide, or, of sufficient extent and prominence to be classified as a range. The Parkway traverses the following ranges: Blue Ridge, Black Mountains, Great Craggies, Pisgah Ledge, Great Balsams, and the Plott Balsams.

Ridge   The term is variously applied but always refers to "a long, sharp edged mountain. Sometimes a ridge makes up a whole mountain and sometimes hits nothin' more'n a spur." Whetstone Ridge, mile 29.4.

Spur   "A long kind of ridge reachin' away from the mountains like a buzzard's wing." The best illustrations are the narrow, winglike projections tapering down from the eastern edge of the Blue Ridge south of Roanoke, Va. Pine Spur, mile 144.8, and High Piney Spur, seen from Fox Hunter's Paradise, mile 218.6.

Top   A descriptive term typical of the Pisgah and Balsam country.

Bottom   "A bottom's the flat land 'longside of a stream below the mountains."

Cove   There are two kinds of coves. One is a small, straight valley down a mountainside. Cove is also applied to an extensive flatland more or less surrounded by mountains. North Cove, seen from Chestoa View, mile 320.7.

Crest line   An imaginary line dividing an elevation, lengthwise, and forming the drainage divide for streams flowing down either side.

Flats   "A flat kind of place some'rs part way up a mountain. The Norvell Flats was big enough fur the South River Lumber Company to yard thur engines." Norvell Flats, mile 34-35.

Gap   "See the outline of that mountain over thar? Them low dips in it's what's knowed as a gap. Some of 'm is whar a road or trail is located acrost the mountains." In general, the Parkway travels the crest line of the Blue Ridge and several other ranges. Therefore, it passes through a long series of gaps and intersects many cross-mountain roads.

Glade   A grassy, open place in the forest. Sections of the high Balsam Mountains, miles 424-442, are referred to as glades because of the grassy areas beneath the stunted wind-spread trees. Glades were also made by Indians, within and below the mountains, by burning large areas of forest for game clearings.

Hollow   "A little hollered out place at the foot of a mountain." Iron Mine Hollow, mile 96.5. Hollows formed at the heads of streams, against a mountainside, have long been favorite cabin sites. The land was level enough for a garden and a corn patch, and close by a spring.

> "I'm goin' to set me down at the head of a holler,
>   An' build me a home sweet home,
> I ketched me a woman, a gun, and a dawg,
>   An' I got no cause to roam."

Levels The levels tell an interesting geological story. These broad mountain summits are believed to be the remnant of an ancient plain uplifted to mountainous heights. Subsequent erosion has dissected much of the levels into ridges and valleys. Big Levels, seen on the left from Greenstone overlook, mile 8.8.

Meadow In the early days the term "meadow" often applied to grassy clearings, many of which lay like bright green patches on a mountainside. The appropriately named Crabtree Meadows Recreation Area, mile 339.3 was formerly known as Blue Ridge Meadows, and, then as now, was visited by groups of picnickers.

Notch A rare term for "gap" in the Southern Highlands. It is typical of New England, as the term "pass" is for the West. Low Notch, mile 239.9.

Pass As used regionally, pass is a rare term referring to a way between the mountains, usually along a stream. In the West a pass refers to a way across the mountains. Goshen Pass, along the Cowpasture River between Lexington and Goshen, Va.

Saddle "Looks jest like it sounds." A saddlelike depression between two high points on a crest line. The Saddle, on Rocky Knob, mile 168.

Slicks, Hells Following a fire, a mountainside with sufficient moisture frequently is covered by an almost impenetrable jungle of rhododendron or mountain laurel. The shiny leaves of the mountain laurel give rise to "ivy slicks" on the steep mountainsides. The jungle-like growths may also be known as "laurel hells," or "ivy hells." Following a burn, dry slopes generally re-cover with the black and Table Mountain pines.

Swag "That's kindly a long, shaller place along the tops of the mountains." Long Swag, mile 433.7.

Valley A long depression between two parallel highlands. In general, they are named for streams that drain them. The Great Valley extends like a trough through the entire Appalachians from New York to Alabama. It is seen west of the Parkway from miles 0 to 100. Since the Great Valley is drained by several rivers, portions of it have regional or local names. The Shenandoah Valley is that portion drained by the Shenandoah River. A large valley has several inlet valleys, just as a large river has several tributaries. Arnolds Valley, mile 78, leads from the Blue Ridge into the Great Valley.

Branch "Ever heard tell of branch water? Nothin' like it. Comes fresh out of a spring and then sort of branches into a bigger waters."

Fork "Lots of mountain streams fork together at the bottom of some mountain. Each one's called a fork." Pisgah Ledge country, miles 412-23.

Prong "About the same as a fork, but mostly smaller. Prongs mostly feed into forks." Pisgah Ledge country, miles 412-23.

Run "A small, feeder stream that makes a beeline scoot down the mountain.'' Big Spy Run. Flows below Big Spy overlook, to the right, mile 26.4.

Watershed As used regionally, an area in the mountains whose streams fill reservoirs for use by local communities and industries. Asheville Watershed, miles 355-370.

Anywhere along the way you might happen upon Uncle Newt, resting his elbows on a rail fence, smokin' his pipe, and being friendly like.

Lower Linville Falls

Grandfather Mountain, lording it over lesser heights, sets the Parkway's scenic tone. Over the entire distance one dominant mountain, or mountain range, captures the view. Beyond Grandfather, Linville Mountain, long and level crested, extends like a prodigious wall along twenty miles of Parkway. As the Linville grows vague with distance, the arched outline of the Blacks fills the western horizon. The Parkway skirts the spruce-clad Blacks, and Craggy Dome stands like a towering beacon on the route ahead. From the Craggy range the Parkway descends toward Asheville and the French Broad River Valley.

Blowing Rock, N.C.
291.9 miles
elev. 3,600

U.S. 221 and U.S. 321 intersection; Boone, 8 miles north on U.S. 221; Blowing Rock, 2 miles south on U.S. 221; Lenoir 21 miles south on U.S. 321.

Blowing Rock is a modern mountain resort that appeals to family folks, whether they be honeymooners, breadwinners, or grandparents. The comfortable coolness of the village is a matter of pride. The noonday temperature is recorded on the main street and compared to that of New York, Washington, Cincinnati, Charlotte, and Miami.

One pleasant day in early autumn we stopped at Blowing Rock to visit lawyer and surveyor George "Bull" Sudderth, a genial gentleman, large of frame and long of memory. Through the years he has acquired a vast store of authentic history on the Watauga region.

"Blowing Rock," said Mr. Sudderth, "was first called Laurel Ridge. Now, what we call 'laurel' is what you'll find as 'rhododendron' in the botany books. It grows real thick all through here.

"In 1848, W. M. A. Lenoir was instrumental in getting the State of North Carolina to build the Caldwell and Watauga Turnpike, and opened a good way up to the mountains. People from around the town of Lenoir began coming up here to spend some time away from the heat, and it took on the name of Summerville.

"One of the first residents to give lodging was William Morris, a local storekeeper. Some young people from Lenoir came and asked him to put them up for a spell. Morris said the men would have to sleep in the garret above the storeroom, while the girls could have the bedroom. They said that would be all right and two of the men asked him to set a price. 'Well,' said Morris, 'I'll bed and board you a month for $8 apiece.' The two men stole a look at each other, hardly believing their good fortune. Morris caught their glance but mistook the meaning. 'But that includes washing.'

"Somewheres about that time the name changed to Blowing Rock. That's the big rock, you know, where the wind's always blowing."

Plateau Rim	eastern hemlock	sweet birch	flame azalea
293.3 miles	chestnut oak	red maple	rosebay
elev. 3,865	red oak	witch hazel	rhododendron
View of Blowing	white oak	serviceberry	greenbriar
Rock, N.C.	white ash	mountain	cinnamon fern
	yellow poplar	winterberry	hay-scented fern

The Blue Ridge plateau, a rolling ramble of forest and fields, rims abruptly at the escarpment edge, with only the sky beyond. Within the interwoven hills and hollows of the plateau lies the garden village of Blowing Rock, a summer haven born of mountain climate and scenery.

Mountains are also the birthplace of rivers. Within the broad survey of your view, four rivers commence their separate ways to the Gulf of Mexico or to the Atlantic Ocean.

From springs on Flat Top Mountain, directly behind you, the New River is born. Its headwaters drain the green hills below and flow away northward alongside the Parkway. The waters of the New River travel far: from here, they pass into West Virginia, meet the Kanawha, then flow into the Ohio, the Mississippi, and ultimately reach the Gulf.

Another Gulf-bound stream, the Watauga, heads in the highlands on the far right. Through rock-bound gorges it hastens to feed the Holston and the Tennessee rivers.

The plateau rim defines the Blue Ridge crest, forming the drainage divide between the Atlantic and the Gulf of Mexico. On the left the Yadkin begins its deep descent into the piedmont. On the right the Johns River dips from the rim and pell-mells southward where it joins the Catawba and other streams en route to the Atlantic Ocean near Charleston.

Moses H. Cone Memorial Park
293-295.5 miles
3,517 acres

Naturalist program: nature walks, local lore demonstrations; Parkway Craft Center; rest rooms; horseback and carriage riding; hiking; fishing in 22-acre Bass Lake and 16-acre Trout Lake.

Moses H. Cone (1857-1908) came east from Tennessee to launch a successful business career that included ventures in New York and the Carolinas.

In 1897 Cone began to acquire the present park area, and during the turn of the century completed Flat Top Manor. The manor now houses the Parkway Craft Center, which is operated by the Southern Highlands Handicraft Guild. Authentic mountain handicrafts such as hooked rugs, pottery, furniture, paintings, handwoven materials, and basketry are on sale or exhibit. Throughout the travel season various skilled handicrafters demonstrate their particular arts at the center.

An information Center occupies a room next to the Craft Center. Some of the implements of yesteryear, whereby the provident mountain folk made their living, are stored here. Selected items from the Frances L. Goodrich collection were once displayed here. Miss Goodrich, daughter of a Presbyterian minister, came to the Southern Highlands in 1895 on mission work from her home in Cleveland, Ohio. She was among the first to inspire the present "renaissnance" of handicraft now perpuated by the Guild.

A checkered coverlet, once draped across the wall, represents a cherished memento. Done in the old-timey golden "Double Bowknot" pattern, it was handwoven by a mountain neighbor of Miss Goodrich and given to her as a gesture of friendship. The kindly deed gave her the idea of encouraging the isolated womenfolk of the mountains to brighten up their often drab existence by engaging in various handicrafts. She in turn opened a retail outlet, the Allanstand, which she gave to the Guild in 1931.

SPINNING WHEEL

There is a deserved regard for items that are handmade and more so if they are done by one individual from start to finish. Time and again, a craftsman masters the fundamentals and evolves into an artist.

Doris Ulman composed and created her pictures with an unwieldy tripod camera with its glass plates and hood, with painstaking care in posing, framing, exposure time, and developing. Her subjects were moulded by their livelihood to be patient and persevering. The weather-board gray of the unpainted cabins and sheds form a background for the weathered features of the wool carder and the basket maker. Mr. Stewart, hewing a log with the broad ax, is steady but not in a hurry. The young woman churning butter shows the weariness of age coming too soon. No need to hurry. Work is never done.

Doris Ulman photographed these highlands and their people in 1933-34. She died in 1934 and did not live to see the images on some of her finest negatives. But she knew what was there the second she squeezed the shutter bulb.

Filling the bottom of a broad basin below the Craft Center lies Bass Lake, a lovely blue gem spangled with water lillies. Nearby Trout Lake is a short distance north across the Parkway motor road.

YELLOW POPLAR OR TULIP TREE

Each lake is surrounded with bridle paths and carriage roads, part of the 26 miles of wander-ways that roam in a delightfully casual manner through the park. They are also available to the hiker.

The trails extend between and over Flat Top and Rich Mountains. The way passes through virgin forest: giant hemlock and yellow poplar.

EASTERN OR CANADIAN HEMLOCK

Flat Top Mountain first enters into our country's literature following the explorations of August Gottlieb

WHITE-TAILED DEER

Spangenberg, a Moravian bishop. In the winter of 1752 the bishop led a group into western Carolina to select the site for a colony. Reaching the summit of Flat Top he observed "hundreds of mountain peaks all around" presenting a "spectacle like ocean waves in a storm." Though the Moravians left the mountains and settled the founding site of Winston-Salem, the good Bishop's observation of the mountains still rings true.

The dark, rich soil is the reason for Rich Mountain's name. A bridle trail winds up its slopes from Trout Lake, through the old deer park. Northern white-tailed deer were stocked within a spacious fenced area for a number of years and then released. Mr. Cone was an avid conservationist. At that time, in the early 1900s, deer were as rare in this vicinity as hen's teeth.

Ground flowers flourish beneath the forest on Rich Mountain. One of the most interesting is the ginseng, or "sang." The root of this plant is in great demand by "old-fashioned" Chinese and others who believe it has wondrous powers. Their reason is based primarily on the fact that the forked root has the sign, or shape, of a man. Therefore, it must be a source of male virility and well being. Needless to say, the mountaineers do not put much faith in the belief or they wouldn't sell the "sang."

The forest and shrub cover of Cone Park contains a greater number of species than any other recreation area along the Parkway. The reasons are twofold. The park contains a variety of environments and the Cones introduced many species of particular appeal to them. The most outstanding of these is the honor guard of Fraser fir recruited from the high, native peaks to stand in sentinel rows beside the grave of Mr. and Mrs. Cone. The family grave lies on the slopes of Flat Top, a short distance above the craft center.

GINSENG OR "SANG"

Mr. Cone did not live many years to appreciate the estate he toiled so diligently to complete. True, his prize apple orchards won several firsts at top fairs throughout the country, and he enjoyed several summers of fishing, horseback riding, and social living. But the memories of those twenty-five-mile up-mountain hauls by ox teams to bring materials for the manor still seemed like yesterday.

FRASER FIR

After the death of Mrs. Cone, the estate was transferred to the National Park Service in 1950, "to be used as a park and pleasuring ground in perpetuity in order to make a lasting memorial to Moses H. Cone."

Julian Price Memorial Park
295.5-300 miles
3,900 acres

Naturalist program: amphitheater, nature walks; campgrounds; picnic grounds; rest rooms; hiking trails; trout fishing; boat rental.

The wilderness appeal of forested highlands and cold mountain streams welcomes the camper, hiker, and fisherman. Julian Price, for whom the Park is named, acquired

Moses H. Cone Recreation Area and Mansion

the land during the late thirties and early forties with the intention of creating a superb vacation haven for the employees of the Jefferson Standard Life Insurance Company. These plans were forestalled by his untimely death in 1946. Jefferson Standard donated the area to the National Park Service for public use, requesting that Boone Fork be dammed to form Price Lake as a memorial.

Julian Price Memorial Park is gradually reverting to a forested wilderness. The present area formed part of a huge tract harvested of its timber in 1912-1930 by William S. Whiting, the lumber baron.

CHESTNUT

Before that time a tall virgin forest of chestnut, yellow poplar, and hemlock covered the cool, moist hills and hollows. Of the three prime originals, yellow poplar, or tulip tree, is making a good recovery. The chestnut has fallen victim to a fungus blight. Hemlock, now that its attractive seedlings are protected by the National Park Service, will probably regain its former numbers. Other common hardwoods are the oak, ash, birch, and maple.

WHITE ASH

The forest must have been a beauty to see. The memory of it brings a tone of reverence to the eyes of "Bull" Sudderth. "Beat anything you ever saw," says Bull, so named by his companions for the way he "bulled" through the brush. "It was the best boundary of timber in Carolina. I think Whiting cut thirty million feet there, maybe more. There were poplars six feet through. We were out fishing and saw one cut down there on Boone Fork. We figured it was a hundred feet to the first limb.

"The chestnut got to a mighty size too. We was sitting on this stump over on Chestnut Knob. Oh, I'd say it was eight feet through, and we got to figuring how old it was. We got to counting the rings. I forget just how many, but it was close to three hundred."

Bull Sudderth once owned several tracts of land now in the Park. One includes Bull Mountain, rising a few hundred feet above the motor road, south of mile 296. "The original name before I owned it was Strawberry Mountain. They still come out thick every spring in some of them old fields."

Near mile 295, just within the boundary of Moses H. Cone Memorial Park, are the Raven Rocks where Bull Sudderth and his fellow townsmen often climbed to view the landscape. "That's one of the prettiest places in the country. The ravens used to build there in the spring of the year. I've seen 'em when I was a boy. Law, they raised there for years, great droves of them. They were awful bad about young lambs and pecking their eyes out. We'd slip up there to the rocks and fire into them. We never killed many, just shot to run 'em off. They're a wilderness bird and don't stay long once a place becomes much settled."

The forested acres of Julian Price Memorial Park have never been a much settled place. Jesse Boone, a nephew

BLACK BEAR

of the famous Daniel (1734-1820), built the first cabin and farmed a small patch by Boone Fork, the stream bearing his name. He came in 1810 and left in 1817.

It would be an adventure brought to life if old Daniel himself had fished and hunted along the shaggy shores of Boone Fork. Perhaps he did. During the 1760s, when he lived on the Yadkin River below the Blue Ridge, Daniel made many hunting sorties into the mountains, probably some of his favorite hunting haunts.

The surrounding wilds were well known to a famous hunter of a later generation, Harrison Aldrich (1821-1905). Ash Bear Pen Knob, rising above the Parkway at mile 299, was one of several locations where Harrison built a pen, or deadfall, to catch bears. Usually they were made of locust, but ash is a "good, substantial wood that a bear couldn't gnaw his way out of." Ash trees are plentiful on the mountain.

Like other bear hunters of his day, Harrison often went into the bear's cave to drive the animal out. Usually it sought only to escape and would bolt into the open. But one time Harrison "got tore up pretty bad. There wasn't much room for the bear to get out. The bear come out over him and raked him with his claws."

Bull Sudderth doesn't hold too high an opinion of the old time bear hunter. "Men like Harrison stayed in the woods the biggest part of the time. The women folks dug 'sang,' and they hunted. They had lots of hogs they turned loose in the woods and they wouldn't work. These razorback hogs run loose in the woods and, law, they just got fat on acorns and chestnuts. They had good meat on 'em, but it took from three to six years to raise them big enough for killin'. Now you can make a good hog in a year.

"All hogs had a mark of some kind, a cut or notch, usually on the ear. You had to go to Boone and have your mark registered. Law, there was more trouble about people accused of stealing pigs."

A desperate breed of men pilfered many a pig during the Civil War. "Deserters from both armies piled in here because it was a good place to hide. Most of this crowd was what they called bushwhackers, and they wasn't anything. All they wanted to do was slip around and rob."

Most of the local population were of Southern persuasion, but a large minority favored the North. Occasionally small groups slipped through the lines to join the Union forces in Tennessee.

"Right close to Miray Knob on Boone Fork is a place where they hid out. They come and lay out in that rock clift. Their friends fed 'em or they'd slip out and kill somebody's hog, or steal. They was part of the old Keith Blalock gang."

Keith Blalock (1836-1913)—there was a man, hated by many and admired by more than a few. During the war he recruited men for the Union forces and fought numerous small but violent battles with his pro-Southern neighbors.

He joined the Confederate Army, but presumably, merely as a dodge. Accompanied by his wife who enlisted with him as private "Sam" Blalock, he joined Colonel Zebulon Vance's 26th Regiment. A short time thereafter, Keith rubbed himself with poison oak and managed to persuade the army doctors that he had an incurable malady. He was then given his discharge. This accomplished, "Sam" had much less trouble in acquiring hers.

Keith returned home and lived on a remote portion of Grandfather Mountain, meanwhile engaging in pro-Union activities, some of which could be more accurately described as grudge fights. He outlived the war—minus an eye.

The perilous times of Keith are typical of the entire Southern Highlands region during the Civil War. No great battles were fought, but partisan warfare, gang attacks, and cavalry raids all reaped a dreadful booty of misery and destruction.

BLUE JAY

Time has dulled the edge of those memories, even as Julian Price Memorial Park is returning to a forest of giant hardwoods and finally losing, trace by trace, the mark of the lumberman.

Boone Fork pools and frolics through a wealth of green wilderness and Price Lake reflects a quiet blue.

Forest Trees and Shrubs

WOOD THRUSH

Originally a virgin forest of hardwood-conifer dominated by yellow poplar, chestnut, white ash, and hemlock. Some virgin timber remains, particularly in Cone Park. The present forest is returning to its original state except for the chestnut. The abundant white pine above Bass Lake were planted by Mr. Cone. Names common to the region are listed below as well as alternates.

yellow poplar or tulip tree	red oak or water oak	yellow buckeye
Fraser magnolia or wahoo	white oak	shagbark hickory
cucumber tree or cowcumber	chestnut oak	pignut hickory
chestnut sprouts	beech	black walnut
	sweet birch or mahogany	butternut or white walnut
	yellow birch or tough mahogany	red maple

List continues

sugar maple or sugar tree
striped maple (Trout Lake)
basswood or lynn
black locust
black or sour gum
serviceberry or sarvis
black cherry
pin or fire cherry
chokeberry
sourwood
black willow
silky willow
sassafras
mountain winterberry or holly
flame azalea or honeysuckle
menziesia or minniebush

highbush blueberry or huckleberry
black huckleberry or bearberry
cinnamonbush
withe-rod viburnum or shonny haw
hobblebush viburnum (Trout Lake)
American elder
wild hydrangea or quillweed
greenbriar
sweet shrub or bubby bush
flowering dogwood
alternate-leaved dogwood
staghorn sumac
smooth sumac

hawthorn
eastern hemlock or spruce pine
Carolina hemlock or spruce pine
eastern white pine
red spruce or he-balsam (craft center)
Fraser fir or she-balsam (Cone Grave)
witch hazel
rosebay rhododendron or white laurel
Carolina rhododendron (craft center)
catawba rhododendron or red laurel (craft center)

Flowers

large-flowered trillium
lousewort
Solomon's seal
sarsaparilla

ginseng or ''sang''
lyre-leaved sage (Bass Lake)
American bellflower
horsemint

pale touch-me-not
heal-all
white wood aster
white snakeroot

Ferns

lady fern
cinnamon fern

interrupted fern
Christmas fern

hay-scented fern
bracken

Birds

Carolina junco
wood thrush
bluejay
ovenbird

chestnut-sided warbler
black-throated blue warbler

indigo bunting
field sparrow
ruffed grouse

Sims Pond Overlook
295.9 miles
elev. 3,447

The pond is fed by Sims Creek, named for Hamp Sims (1871-1951), a former resident. "He lived on Boone's Fork, and this Sims Creek run through his land. He had a good farm ... growed some stock and drank his dram once in a while. Had ole man Charlie Moody to build his coffin ... had it for years before he died." *(Jim Lyons, Boone, N.C., 1956)*

Sims was very proud of the coffin, as it was made to his own specifications. When it was finished, he drove over to

Charlie Moody's and loaded the huge casket into his Model T Ford. The load was a mite top-heavy and on the way home he failed to make a sharp curve. The car overturned and Hamp and his coffin upended on the road bank. Bruised but undaunted, Hamp sparkled out a few choice comments, then nodded to his coffin and remarked, "Looks like I'm a-goin' to need it afore long."

But Hamp and his wooden friend stayed above the ground for a good while after that. Occasionally he had a whimsical streak and tried it out for size. Snugly inside, he would while away the evening, singing mournful songs.

Hamp liked to say he had it made out of chestnut so he could go through hell a-poppin' and a-crackin'. But Charlie Moody says he made it out of maple.

Price Lake
296.7 miles
Boat rental

Price Lake, 47 acres of cool, mountain headwaters, fulfills the wish of Julian Price. The lake is stocked with trout for the fishermen and hikers who can tromp the edge-forest trails. Campers, or those who pause for a reflective moment, enjoy the lake's blue, liquid loveliness. A man-made touch to enhance the wilderness, its mood varies with the time or with the weather:

RAINBOW TROUT

> Brisk with the tang of morning,
> Sun-spangled in the golden afternoon,
> Dusky with evening's stretching shadows,
> A lisping quiet in the night.

Halloway Mountain Road Exit
298.6 miles

This road leads to U.S. 221.

Tanawha Trail
298–305 miles

Tanawha is Cherokee for hawk or eagle and is the Cherokee name for Grandfather Mountain.

Tanawha Trail meanders 13.5 miles around Grandfather along seven miles of the Parkway between Julian Price Memorial Park and Beacon Heights. There are several leg-stretcher trails leading into Tanawha from intervening parking overlooks. It is fine to hike any time of year; each season has a character of its own.

Now it is late August. But it is not the time for birds. They are not apparent either by sight or sound. One female grosbeak objects from a thicket. It is not a time for mammals. One red squirrel scolds from a low branch, angry squeaks in time with his whiplashing tail. And, along the dryer stretches of terrain, it is not the time for flowers. The Carolina lily stands tall and weary, bearing a pair of seed pods atop its stem. Its wan appearance seems to say "I raised my offspring and now I'm so tired." The yellow buckeye is shedding its

FEATHER SYMBOL OF THE
TANAHWA TRAIL

leaves. Now and then a shriveled leaf drifts quietly to the ground. The mosses are brown and stiff. The lichens curl dryly on the rocks.

But there is always a time for something. Bright spots of red and an occasional blue peek from the forest floor and undergrowth. Late August is harvest time when brightly colored fruits appear. An egg-shaped bundle of red berries is the bright result of a Jack-in-the-pulpit, its leaves wilted from its stalk. A single red berry identifies a trillium, also on a leafless stalk. Loose, flat-topped clusters of red berries on red stems grow among the heart-shaped leaves of the hobblebush viburnum. At closer look, an occasional berry has turned purple. Here on the trail lies a coral-pink cone of the Frazer magnolia. Bright red seeds are pushing into view. At the foot of a rock outcrop, cobalt blue berries rise on the foot-high stalks of bead lilies.

Life is greener and more robust where a stream passes beneath a foot bridge. The wet rocks are veneered with moss and liverwort. Here, the flowers of August are alive and well. The stream's edge is bordered by pink turtlehead and orange jewelweed. The rich soil of the trailside cove is productive of tall, straight trees and a flourishing ground cover. Flat, white clusters crown the white snakeroot. White spikes of black cohosh wave wandlike atop their leaves. Yellow coneflower and scarlet Oswego tea crowd both sides of the path. Ferns are locally abundant, but only the American shield fern retains its robust vigor, three feet high and abounding among the rocks.

A sound is heard, a lazy, sleepy sound. You pause. It comes again. You listen for more. The sound becomes more awake and frequent. It's a katydid tuning up. "Dih dih dih dit." Soon the player is joined by another. For a while you can locate the players by ear, but identity is soon lost in numbers, the sounds merging into a symphony of sorts, a staccato of stridulating wings.

It is twilight and time to leave the trail. **8-21-87**

View of **Calloway Peak** 299.7 miles elev. 3,798	*tulip tree* *sassafrass* *chestnut oak* *black birch*	*red oak* *hemlock* *rosebay* *rhododendron*	*sourwood* *red maple* *black gum* *Dutchman's pipe*

An "over-your-shoulder" view of Calloway Peak, nosing up far right to the south. Calloway Peak, 5,964 feet, is the highest point on Grandfather Mountain, and the highest altitude of the Blue Ridge Range.

Two rock outcrops known to geologists as "whalebacks" protrude in front of the overlook. They develop where exposed bedrock is inclined at a moderate angle to that of the existing slope and are gradually rounded and humpbacked by the peeling and decomposing effects of weathering water and ice.

Boone Fork Parking Area
300 miles
elev. 3,900

Access to Tanawha Trail and privately-owned Grandfather Mountain Trail System where a hiking permit is required. Boone Fork Creek, a melody of riffles, crosses under a foot bridge and the Parkway.

An Ode to the Chestnut

Green Mountain Overlook
300.6 miles
elev. 4,134

The chestnut blight struck the mountain forest in the late 1920s and early 30s and all but eliminated the chestnut throngs that covered entire slopes. The blight is a fungus disease introduced inadvertently to the New York City Herbarium from chestnut trees brought from the Orient. In less than a decade the native trees were eliminated with the thoroughness of a forest fire.

The loss hit the mountain economy like a plant-closing in a small town. Gone were the multiple uses of its lumber and gone were the nuts that fed hogs and cattle and served as a much relied-upon "cash-crop" in a land of barter. Dead, standing trees persevered among the "take-over" forest into the 50s, and provided the best rails for fences. This was the presumed death knell of the chestnut.

But the chestnut is stubborn and clings to life. A remnant few persist in the surrounding forest. Most originate as sprouts from the roots of mature trees long since deadened by the blight and decayed away. Some chestnuts reach a height of 20 or 30 feet; a pathetic contrast of vigorous, green-leaved shoots and forlorn branches of brown, shriveled crisps.

The battle is not lost. At least one intact stand still exists in Michigan. Seedlings are being introduced into former habitats. Perhaps the blight and the chestnut can effect a peaceful co-existence.

Pilot Ridge Overlook
301.8 miles
elev. 4,400

The overlook is located at Pilot Ridge, long and steep sided, extending from afar at the base of Grandfather, up to Calloway Peak. The view, front left, looks into the Globe, a huge, unruly hollow, so named by Bishop Spangenberg, founder of the Moravian church in America. The bishop and his party reconnoitered the mountains in 1752, apparently intending to ascend the Blue Ridge by way of a known traversable route along the Yadkin River valley. Instead they wandered southward into the rough, broken country seen below.

The explorers completed their journey and safely returned to their settlement near Charlottesville. But at times they feared and wondered. "Part of the way we had to crawl on hands and feet; sometimes we had to take baggage and saddles and the horses and drag them up the mountains for the horses were in danger of falling backwards as we once had an experience. And sometimes we had to pull the horses up while they trembled and quivered like leaves." (*from the journal of Bishop August Gottlieb Spangenberg*).

View of Wilson Creek Valley
302.2 miles
elev. 4,356

The northern reach of the Pisgah National Forest lies below, an ocean of turbulent terrain covered with tranquil, green forest. And my, how the wind can blow, as though you were sea-borne and sailing before the mast.

Rough Ridge Parking Area
302.9 miles
elev. 4,293

red spruce	*black birch*	*rosebay rhododendron*
Fraser fir	*black cherry*	*striped maple*
hemlock	*yellow birch*	*witch hazel*
tulip tree	*red maple*	

A leg-stretcher trail heads up to a footbridge overlooking a small stream bordered with umbrella leaf and pink turtlehead. The path connects to the Tanawha Trail. Southward leads to shrubby, wind-buffeted Rough Ridge. Northward leads through a shaded mix of fern-covered rocks and rich, moist coves dense with wild flowers. The trees grow tall and sturdy, gradually regaining the girth and height known before the forest was gleaned of timber in the early 1900s.

Given the protection of the National Park Service and the Grandfather Mountain Company, these slopes may resume the character they had two centuries ago when they were explored by Andre and François Michaux. Father and son, they were sent by the French government, 1785–97, to study and collect native plants. The younger Michaux returned alone in 1802.

Separately and together they traveled, observed, noted, and collected the length and breadth of the new United States. The writings of the son reflect the love of both for the North Carolina Mountains, including one he called Greatfather Mountain.

A walk along the Tanawha Trail is very like the experiences and observations related by the younger Michaux—

On the long-leaved cucumber tree or Frazer magnolia: "I have no where found it more abundant as on the steepest part of the lofty mountains of North Carolina, particularly those which are called by the inhabitants Great Father Mountains, Black and Iron Mountains. . . . The soil of these mountains, which is brown and deep, and of an excellent quality, is peculiarly favorable to its growth . . . the flowers are 3 or 4 inches in diameter, of a fine white color. . . . The cones are oval, 3 or 4 inches long and . . . of a beautiful rose color when ripe."

On the mountain laurel: "I have no where seen it more profusely multiplied, than in North Carolina, on the loftiest part of the Alleghenies. It occupies tracts of more than 100 acres, and forms upon the summit, and for a third of the distance down the sides, thickets of 18 or 20 feet in height, which are rendered nearly impenetrable by the crooked and unyielding trunks, crossed and locked with each other. As the shrubs which compose these copses are of an uniform height and richly laden with evergreen foliage, they present, at a distance, the appearance of verdant meadows, surrounded by tall trees."

On the big or yellow buckeye: "I have seen no situations that appear more favourable to the Big Buckeye than the declivities of the lofty mountains of North Carolina, and particularly of the Greatfather Mountain, the Iron Mountain and the Black Mountain, where the soil is generally deep, loose, and fertile. The coolness and humidity which reign in these elevated regions, appear likewise to be necessary to its utmost expansion; it here towers to the height of 60 or 70 feet, with a diameter of 3 or 4 feet, and is considered as proof of the richness of the forest. . . . The flowers (are) of a light, agreeable yellow. . . ." The buckeye is, "One of the earliest to cast its leaves; they begin to fall about the 15th of August."

The words of Michaux accompany the Tanawha Trail and bring a regard to keep it as it is.

> Lay no hand on the flower
> Leave the moss as it lies
> Leave the forest to bird song
> Touch it only with your eyes.

Yonahlossee Overlook
303.9 miles
elev. 4,412

The muted sounds of tire squeals and car engines playing "musical gears" convey the presence of the Yonahlossee Trail, a fifteen-mile section of U.S. 221 traversing Grandfather Mountain just below but hidden by the forest.

The name derives from the Cherokee for bear track, or passing bear.

The Linville Improvement Company acquired a charter to build an eighteen-mile toll road, or turnpike, between Linville and Blowing Rock in 1890 and completed it a few years later. Tolls were collected until approximately 1925 when the road became part of the state highway system.

Workmen labored ten hours with pick and shovel for a daily wage of seventy-five cents. The total cost of construction came to $18,000. Today the distance of good mountain road built by that amount could be measured in feet—or inches.

Stage coaches traveled the turnpike for a few years

but soon gave way to the era of the Model T. In its day, few roads equaled the Yonahlossee as a scenic route. A writer of an earlier day, when poetic extravagance was a conscientious art, describes it as "traversing the entire south slope of Grandfather Mountain, a region as rugged as if Vulcan's mighty anvils had been thrown from the throttles of a volcano and lodged in the mountain side. High up the imposing crags the eye is diverted into great dark holes and hollows that Sol's rays have never penetrated; but in the opposite direction, the expansive view is extended far into the blue haze of the sunny South." (Dugger: *Balsam Groves of Grandfather Mountain*).

Linn Cove
Parking Area
304.4 miles
elev. 4,315

Information station; comfort station; trail to view of Linn Cove Viaduct linking with Tanawha Trail.

The name Linn Cove is of Scottish derivation. A Linn refers variously to a craggy precipice or to falling or pooling water along a steep mountain side. A cove is a hollow in a rock formation or a cave. The terms are as appropriate here as in the Scottish Highlands.

Linn Cove Viaduct

The Linn Cove Viaduct, completed in 1983, is part of the final 7½ miles of motor road opened to parkway visitors. The viaduct is a symbol of pride to the problem-solving construction engineer and brings his science into rapport with Michaelangelo.

All aspects of planning and construction were designed to protect the rugged beauty of Grandfather Mountain. Most bridge-type construction along a mountain would be projected on a straight line. Interfering portions of the mountain would be blasted away to facilitate the bridge. Not so at Grandfather. The viaduct is adapted to the existing contours and becomes a part of the mountain rather than a feature in itself. Someone once said, "Great art conceals art," and so it is with the Grandfather and the viaduct.

The viaduct is a quarter mile long, formed horizontally by 153 precast segments of reinforced concrete, each 8.6 feet long and weighing 50 tons. The viaduct is supported on seven vertical piers at spans of 180 feet.

Segments were formed in a casting site about a mile away. The casting of each segment was controlled by computer to conform with complete accuracy to the S-shaped, banking design of the viaduct. No two segments have the same dimensions and only one segment is straight.

Construction commenced at the southern end and

progressed northward segment by segment. Each segment was delivered by truck driven backwards over the completed portion of the viaduct. A "stiff-leg" crane then hoisted the segment over the edge of the construction and supported it as it was being secured into the previous segment.

In this manner, the horizontal construction extended armlike over the ground to a maximum distance of 90 feet. A temporary steel brace supported the viaduct at this point and assembly continued another 90 feet at which point a permanent vertical support pier was assembled by lowering segments onto a preconstructed base and working up to join into the superstructure.

The base of each pier is of reinforced concrete faced with granite. Drilling, to prepare for the secure anchoring of the pier base, was the only construction activity conducted on the ground. Otherwise, all construction and assembly was on or from the viaduct, moving segment by segment, pier by pier, to completion.

Riding the veering, graceful curves of the viaduct is like the flight of a soaring hawk. Like Tanawha.

Stack Rock Parking Area
304.8 miles
elev. 4,286

An access into Tanawha Trail leads northward a short distance to where Stack Rock pokes up from the slopes below. This local "curiosity" has served as a landmark for generations of hunters and hikers. The cracked and jointed appearance of this free-standing chimney formation gives the appearance of several large rocks stacked one on top of the other.

Beneath the Shaggy Brows of Grandfather Mountain

On September 11, 1987 an event was held on Grandfather Mountain marking the final union of the Blue Ridge Parkway. The event celebrated a history that began over half a century ago. Its origin was humble and worthy, a work project to combat the Great Depression and bring employment to an impoverished land. Mountain men, eager for work, toiled with pick and shovel, the ax, and the crosscut saw to clear the way for the motor road, for hiking trails, and for picnic grounds.

Through the years, obedient to the plans of the landscape architect and the blueprints of the engineer, they mastered the skills for operating bulldozers, cranes, tractors, dumptrucks, and jackhammers. They built bridges, blasted tunnels, and transplanted rhododendron and mountain laurel.

Through the years, their lives and the lives of their children improved with the building and maintaining of the Parkway. They remembered homes of weatherboard gray and the kerosene lamp. Now they were long accustomed to the comforts of the red brick ranch and more.

September 11, 1987 was their day. They gathered

and listened to the speeches of the superintendents, the politicians, and the influential citizens. And they nodded in happy agreement, grinning to hear those pretty words about what they were so proud to be a part of.

And all beneath the shaggy brows of Grandfather Mountain.

One of the honored guests, "beneath the shaggy brows of Grandfather Mountain," on September 11, 1987, was a delighted octogenarian, Sam P. Weems. He came to the Parkway in 1935 commencing his National Park Service career acquiring land for Rocky Knob and other recreation areas. He served as Parkway Superintendent, 1944-1966. During his long tenure he planned and "politicked" on behalf of his beloved Blue Ridge Parkway with a will, a purpose, and a natural skill. That September day on Grandfather Mountain was his to cherish above all others.

View from Beacon Heights
305.2 miles
elev. 4,212
leg-stretcher trail

Hiking has long been a hobby in America. The more adventurous hikers like to travel the little known and far away. Two of the most inspiring incentives are to seek and discover mountain views and to walk along untrod ways.

During the 1890s, a foot-voyaging poet named A. M. Huger traveled the mountains, particularly from Grandfather to the Linville Gorge. "One of them summer fellers," the mountaineers said, and knew him for miles around as "Hu-gee." Huger gave himself the sobriquet of "Chucky Joe," and delighted in laying out new trails and naming new places. He carried a hatchet to chop his way and a stone chisel with which he chiseled his nickname in certain rocks. He frequently named outstanding features and views, and painted the name on a sign for passersby.

Chucky Joe enjoyed the view from a smooth quartzite outcrop that curved down the mountainside, and named the site Beacon Heights.

No fairer land surely than this, where the hills
Are feathered with forests, and braided with rills!
The mountains that over these green valleys rise
Ever woo'd by the winds, ever kissed by the skies;
And the homes and the hearts that they shelter shall hold
Gifts sweeter than glory and richer than gold.
(A.M. Huger)

The Parkway trail, near its entrance onto the view site, merges with an old footpath, barely apparent. Could it be the mark of Chucky Joe?

From the parking area, the trail to the view passes through a dark green aisle-way of rosebay rhododendron and mountain laurel. Red spruce and hemlock poke above here and there. The ground cover reflects the cool environment: galax, speckled wood lily, teaberry, wild lily of the valley, and painted trillium.

GALAX

Seemingly out of place are the Fraser magnolia trees with their large leaves and languid appearance so reminiscent of the tropics.

The trail ends at Beacon Heights, a view-platform of bare quartzite. Before you spread the stream-carved foothills of the Blue Ridge. The weird outline on the far right points out the Linville Falls area. The "Big Nose" mountain, though you'd never believe it, is Table Rock seen from an unusual angle. Hawksbill nudges close behind.

Farther to the right, back of neighborly Grandfather Mountain, lies the forest-filled Linville River Valley, with the Black range looming big and long against the horizon.

The Thin, Moist World of the Salamander

Drought is unknown in these mountains. The high peaks capture rain clouds and keep them as fogs and mists that permeate moisture into the soil. Water moves gradually and constantly down the slopes through the shallow, spongy sod.

SALAMANDER

Moisture that may evaporate during the day condenses and returns during the night. The result is a stable temperature and humidity that is most constant in the surface inches of soil or rocks.

These few inches of living veneer are the world of the salamander. Native salamanders are primarily of the family Plethodontidae, or salamanders with abundant teeth. They inhabit every ecological niche keyed to the surface area or just beneath it. They live beneath the leaf mold, under or between rocks, in rotted logs, in springs and waterways. They are small, long-tailed, four-legged creatures, ranging in length from two to seven inches. The females lay gelatinous-covered eggs about the size of BBs. Some species curl protectively around their eggs, probably to keep them moist. Other species adhere them to rocks under water. The Plethodonts are lungless. The adults breathe through their skins and through membranes in their mouths.

Salamanders, like frogs, are amphibians. As such, larval forms hatching from the eggs breathe by means of gills. Unlike the frog, however, the Plethodonts do not have an obligatory aquatic stage. The larvae may thrive on land or water. Some species pass their entire larval stage in the egg and emerge as adults.

Most of the known species of Plethodonts occur in the Appalachians, giving credence that the Appalachians are their site of origin. Also, the most primitive as well as the most specialized forms are found in this region.

All Plethodonts are believed to be descended from a common ancestor wherein different species developed by adapting to different environments within the aforementioned living veneer. The process is still active as evidenced by hybridizing within species. And that's the way life is, trying to adapt to the world as it finds it.

Of the Plethodonts, the Yonahlossee salamander has specialized as a burrower, squirmily digging long tunnels under the forest floor that open covertly beneath a log or a piece of bark. The Yonahlossee is black with a dorsal band of chestnut that matches the ochre of rotted logs.

The black-bellied salamander frequents shady mountain cascades, lying at the base of boulders or along the banks and ready to plop out of sight.

The pigmy salamander lives at the highest elevations, up to 6,500 feet, beneath stones, logs, and mosses of the spruce-balsam forests.

And among rock crevices and crannies the lead-colored Metcalf's salamander observes the night with bulging, frog-like eyes, and with slow and silent deliberation stalks its insect prey.

Grandmother Gap
306.2 miles
elev. 4,051

A direct but rough trail through Grandmother Gap, dating at least to the time of the pioneers, connected the eastern lowlands with the Toe River Valley. It ascended through some of the roughest terrain in the Blue Ridge. In the Toe River Valley the trail joined the Yellow Mountain Road, a main pioneer artery between Carolina and Tennessee.

Grandfather Mountain Overlook
306.6 miles
elev. 4,154

Grandfather Mountain represents the climax of the Blue Ridge in height and grandeur. The long slopes incline to a sharp, jagged crest line of dark, gray rock. The profile of a grandfather is outlined along the summit. His nose is Calloway Peak, 5,938 feet, the high point of the Blue Ridge. The name, however, probably comes from a stone face on the high slopes resembling an aged patriarch.

The Grandfather is composed of quartzite, one of the most durable rocks known. The region along the Parkway between mileposts 284 and 317 is largely a quartzite area surrounded by an older rock formation. Geologists tell us that a great mass of this older rock overrode the quartzite during a period of gradual but tremendous earth movement millions of years ago. It has since been eroded away by time and the elements, revealing the quartzite. The durability of this rock is a principal reason for the towering height of the Grandfather.

Although a mere jaunt in comparison to a conquest of Mt. Everest or the Matterhorn, climbing Grandfather is not done without valor or strain. The French botanist and world traveler, André Michaux, climbed it in August of 1794. The enthusiastic entry in his journal reads, "Climbed to the summit of the highest mountain of all North America, and with my companion and guide, sang the Marseilles Hymn, and cried, 'Long live America and the French Republic! Long live Liberty'!"

Although he knew nothing of the great western peaks, Michaux had seen the Black Mountains, whose high point

exceeds the Grandfather's by more than 700 feet, but he believed his eyes and the opinions of the local mountaineers. Several of their present-day descendants still claim Grandfather is the highest in the east and "pay no mind to them scientific gadgets."

Michaux came to the United States in the service of the French government to collect native plants for the nurseries in Paris. He found a great reward on Grandfather with its abundance and variety. Asa Gray, the father of American botany, came in 1841 to study in the footsteps of the revered Michaux. Gray named several of the native plants after the French pioneer and included them in his *Manual of Botany*.

During Gray's visit to Grandfather he may well have been guided by two hunters, a father and son named James and Harrison Aldrich. The son, known by the colorful salute of "Rollingbumb," killed over a hundred bears. The luckless quarry was not even safe in its den, for Rollingbumb went in and drove it out.

Aldrich had a woodsman's love for the big mountain, a feeling that is held in common by countless highlanders today. Each June, since 1924, they come by the thousands to Grandfather for the annual "Singing on the Mountain." The roads are full of cars for miles away and the green slopes of the mountain are converted into an outdoor cathedral by droves of latter-day pilgrims who come to sing and worship. This religious and social event was founded by Uncle Joe Hartley, a loyal booster of Grandfather who attended the singing every year until his death in 1966.

Since 1956, the Grandfather has been host to a romantic and colorful gathering of the Scottish clans. The clansmen are predominantly descendants of highlanders who settled in the Carolina piedmont.

As though they were on the grassy slopes below Ben Nevis, the Campbells, MacLeods, Stewarts, MacDonalds, and MacRaes set up their tartan standards and engage in tryouts to represent their clan in the highland fling, sword dance, bagpipes, tossing the caber, and various other events. The martial skirling of the pipes and drums puts a wild tingle in the veins and makes mustered-out infantrymen feel like making a charge.

Today you may drive by toll road from U.S. 221 almost to the mountain summit and from there enjoy a "vibrating" view from the "Swinging Bridge," securely moored between two peaks of the Grandfather.

The Hang Gliders

They circle slowly above Grandfather Mountain on brightly colored dacron sails. Two hang gliders spiral upward on rising drafts of warm air, or thermals. Their air speed is skillfully controlled, just enough to prevent stalling. Conditions are optimum for remaining aloft. The wind is calm, with a large area free of turbulence above the east face of Grandfather.

We are witnessing competition in the Masters of Hang Gliding Championships. The winner of the meet (September 7, 1980) is twenty-one-year-old Steve Moyes of Sydney, Australia.

Hang gliding is a new and growing sport that germinated in the California hills during the sixties and is now worldwide. Hang gliders trace their lineage to many near-achievers of the past. Let's include Daedalus and Icarus of Greek mythology, Leonardo da Vinci of the Renaissance, and, of course, Germany's Otto Lilienthal of a century ago. But the man who got them off the ground is America's Dr. Francis M. Rogallo who developed "the Rogallo Flexwing" in the 1940s. Hang gliders may feel like birds, but aerodynamically their wing to the sky is more like a kite.

The Parkway has two hang glider launching sites, by permit only: Ravens Rocks, mile 10.7, and Roanoke Mountain, mile 120.3.

Grandmother Mountain
307.4 miles
elev. 4,063
Parking area

Grandmother Mountain snuggles close to the ponderous shoulders of the Grandfather, like an old woman next to her venerable spouse.

The parking area rests on the west slope of the mountain, surrounded by an amazingly dense understory of rosebay rhododendron. Beneath their blanketing leaves it is never brighter than twilight.

Few plants can grow under such a thicket, but the open border by the parking area invites the tiny purple bluet to bloom a lavender trail during the summertime.

Flat Rock Parking Area
308.3 miles
elev. 3,987

Self-guiding nature trail; mountain-sighting device.

A first impression along the trail is a lush forest growth. The ground is covered with ferns and herbs. Shrubs like the flame azalea, witch hazel, and mountain winterberry approach the stature of trees.

The trees have tall, straight trunks that ascend boldly. But their high branches are curiously trimmed like a giant hedge. Seasonally violent winds keep them cropped to a smooth "windline."

The trail enters the Flat Rock, a sloping quartzite outcrop on the west side of Grandmother Mountain. Flat Rock is similar to the outcrop at Beacon Heights consisting of gray quartzite crisscrossed with "stringers" of white quartz. But it is obviously more weatherworn. Numerous shrubs form encroaching islands that seek to engulf it. The winds, however, keep them at bay. During storms plants are often ripped away, revealing the rock, cleaned and scoured.

AZALEA

The view looks into the Linville River Valley. Below are the blue eye of Lake Kawahna and the fairways of Linville golf course. The Grandfather crowns the horizon on the far right.

Through this intermountain valley the shrill whistle of Tweetsie, the lovable "Iron Horse," once came loud and clear. She puffed along at an unhurried gait between her "stables" in Johnson City, Tenn., and Boone, N. C. Tweetsie never bothered much about her schedule. Who knew when she might have to stop and shoo a cow off the tracks? And in summertime her passengers thought it great fun to hop out and pick wild flowers. Tweetsie stood patiently by, just snorting now and then to keep her steam.

**View of
Lost Cove Cliffs**
*310 miles
elev. 3,812*

Roadside easel: the Brown Mountain Lights.

There are many lost coves in the highlands, isolated inlets extending far into the mountains. This one lies beneath the steep walls of Lost Cove Cliffs.

The view is one of several along the Parkway between Blowing Rock and Linville Mountain where the Brown Mountain Lights may be seen. At night, bright starlike lights sparkle low in the sky. They increase in brilliance and then fade away. Shortly thereafter they reappear. The odd performance continues all night long.

Brown Mountain, a low foothill not seen from the overlook, is innocently involved in the odd phenomenon.

WITCH HAZEL

The Reverend C. E. Gregory of New York first brought the lights to the world's attention. In 1910 he built a cottage on Rattlesnake Knob, a few miles south of here. His view into the distant Catawba Valley, the same as the view seen here, extended over Brown Mountain.

The Reverend observed the peculiar "now-you-see-it-now-you-don't" feature of the lights and described them to his friends. The appeal of the mystery spread throughout the Catawba Valley and the lights became a household topic. Old-timers suddenly remembered seeing them "since and before the days of the Civil War."

MOUNTAIN HOLLY OR
WINTERBERRY

During the next few years they were seen from an increasing number of sites on the mountains and even from the valley floor. Many observations were made miles apart from the innocently involved Brown Mountain, but the name had become firmly established and applied to every weird illumination seen in the valley.

Popular interest continued to increase and in 1913 D. B. Sterrett of the U.S. Geological Survey came to Brown Mountain to observe the lights and determine their origin. His conclusion that they were from the headlights of locomotives failed to satisfy local expectations.

A few years later a flood inundated the Valley and completely halted movement over the rails. When the lights continued to appear the scoffers had a field day at the expense of science. Nothing so commonplace could possibly be the cause. The lights were bound to be an alchemy of mystery. Something like the will-o'-the-wisp that glows over the marshes, the dancing lights of giant lightning bugs, or light from a source never before known.

At the urgent request of both North Carolina senators, science was prevailed upon to try again. The U.S. Geological Survey sent George R. Mansefield to study the lights during the spring of 1922. He made observations from three locations in the Blue Ridge and arrived at a more thoroughly studied but similar conclusion to that of Mr. Sterrett.

According to Mansefield, the Catawba Valley is shaped like a huge basin, enclosed in an arc of the Blue Ridge on the westerly side and by the low South Mountain range on the opposite side. Each evening air of varying temperatures and, therefore, different densities flows into the basin from the mountains. ''The effect of variations in the density of the atmosphere between the observer and the source of light is at one time to increase and at another time to diminish the intensity of the light.... About 47 percent of the lights that the writer was able to study instrumentally were due to headlights, 33 percent to locomotive headlights, 10 percent to brush fires, and 10 percent to stationary lights.'' The lights seen after the flood were attributed mainly to automobiles.

But imagination, once fired, is not easily quenched, and the pet theories of the citizens remain original and defiant. It has been told that some of the lights occur on nights when Posey Slewfoot, the mythical moonshiner, is brewing a batch of incandescent mountain dew. Others swear they are the spirits of scalped Indians looking for a way back to the Happy Hunting Ground.

N.C. Rt. 181
312 miles

Morganton, 32 miles east; Linville 5 miles north.

Camp Creek Parking Area
315.6 miles
elev. 3,443

Trout stream; Linville River tributary; Atlantic drainage.

white pine	red maple	mountain winterberry
eastern hemlock	rosebay rhododendron	red-twig leucothoe
black or sour gum	mountain laurel	serviceberry
Fraser magnolia		

Camp Creek and the Parkway keep company for three miles southward to this parking area. A short distance below, the stream enters Linville River and joins in the hasty descent through Linville Gorge.

Generations of outdoorsmen may have camped along Camp Creek, but its name is derived from the Camp brothers of Chicago, Illinois, who logged the nearby forest in the early 1900s.

The forest, now part of Pisgah National Forest, was and is excellent for white pine and broadleaf trees. In the foreground is an association typical of the region. The trunks rise above a green maze of rosebay rhododendron and mountain laurel. A trail from the parking area zigzags a short distance beneath the thicket archway to the cool sounds of Camp Creek.

Linville Falls
Recreation Area
316.5 miles
440 acres

Naturalist program: campfire talks, nature walks, self-guide trails; access road south: campgrounds, rest room, trout fishing, hiking, visitor information center, access road north: picnic grounds, rest rooms, trout fishing

A 1.4-mile spur road travels alongside the Linville River to within hiking distance of the falls. En route, you will find the River Bend parking area by the river's edge at mile .4. The fast-flowing Linville has eroded a miniature sandy shoal from its hard quartzite bed. Sycamore, butternut, and ironwood, rare trees in the mountains, shade the riverbanks.

Linville Falls Recreation Area, like many National Park Service lands, was acquired through the philanthropy of John D. Rockefeller, Jr. The falls pour through a forested gorge, pristine and primitive as in the days of the Indian. Tall virgin pine and hemlock rise straight and slender. One trailside white pine approaches 150 feet.

EASTERN OR CANADIAN HEMLOCK

The steep walls of the gorge enclose the Linville River for 12 miles, wherein it descends nearly 2,000 feet before breaking into the open levels of the Catawba Valley. Facing downstream, the gorge is formed by the great stretch of Linville Mountain on the right, and Jonas Ridge, Table Rock, and Hawksbill on the left. The mountains are composed of quartzite, a rock even more durable than the hard gneisses and schists that compose most of the highlands along the Parkway. The strong canyon walls impose a narrow and direct course upon the Linville, in contrast to its leisurely meandering once it leaves the mountains.

The falls originated downstream at the foot of the canyon back during dinosaur days, millions of years ago. During that time a huge crack formed northeasterly along the earth's surface. The region on this side of the break uplifted and formed the steep drop creating the ancestral Linville Falls.

Gradually the falls cut upstream while the river carved the beginning of a gorge, or canyon. Ultimately the river cut about as deeply as it could and commenced to "level out" and widen the canyon floor. Subsequently, the mountains uplifted again and once more the stream cut downward, forming a new, smaller canyon within the bottom of the old. This stream action is in progress today, ever so slowly. Quartzite takes a long time to wear away.

The name of Linville is derived from a tragic exploit that occurred in the summer of 1766. William Linville and his son came from the piedmont to hunt, accompanied by John Williams, a young lad of sixteen. While they slept in their camp near the headwaters of the river, a group of Indians attacked them, killing the Linvilles and severely wounding young Williams.

Left for dead, he crawled to an old horse the Indians had left behind and pulled himself onto its back. For five days he traveled, his leg broken and no food to sustain him other than blackberries. Finally he reached a house in the ''Hollows'' of Surrey, below the Blue Ridge near the state line. The lad recovered and lived a long, full life. The Linvilles never left camp. They probably never saw the now famous falls and gorge that bear their name. But during the ensuing years, untold thousands have come and marveled at the view.

For a long time the region was too rugged for all but the most determined visitors. In his book, *Adventures in the Wilds of United States, 1857,* Lanman describes the falls and declares, ''The scenery around them is as wild as it was 100 years ago. Not even a pathway has been made to guide the tourist.''

ROSEBAY

Perhaps the first person to make trails to the falls was the eccentric mountain lover and poet, A. M. Huger, or ''Chucky Joe.'' He sallied out each morning to cut trails and clear the brush away from fine views, evidently on his own initiative. It is probable that the excellent Park Service trails through the area bear at least the ''mark'' of Chucky Joe from nearly a century ago.

CATAWBA

The trail system leads first to a view of the upper falls, a relatively broad but shallow drop occurring before the water makes its spectacular plunge over the lower falls. From the upper falls the water pours into a pondlike widening and drifts for a lazy moment before it suddenly speeds over a riffle of rocks and spirals out of sight. From a rock shelf you can observe the downward spiral dashing to the lip of the lower falls and plunging into an abrupt drop of thirty feet.

CAROLINA

The plant life by the riverbanks and throughout the gorge includes an abundance of rare species and an overall variety. The stream border between the two falls is one of the few locales in the highlands where you can find the three native rhododendrons growing side by side: the rosebay, catawba, and Carolina. Close by the water's edge are several sweet-scented swamp azaleas. Red chokeberry, yellowroot, ninebark, alder, and the evergreen drooping leucothoe, or dog-hobble, grow from cracks in the rock shelf.

DOGHOBBLE OR DROOPING LEUCOTHOE

The trail to ''balcony views'' of the lower falls passes through virgin forest. In pioneering days the trees were saved from the ax by the inaccessible terrain. Lumbermen of the early 1900s, with the improved methods of their day, could have harvested many a Linville forest giant. But the land belonged to the Hossfield family, ardent conservationists who "wouldn't let a brush be cut." They preserved the forest prior to its acquisition for the National Park Service.

The forest along the trail is composed of a surprisingly few species of trees. Through years of competition the trees best adapted to this area have won out and excluded all others. Here, then, is a climax forest. The Carolina hemlocks are probably among the largest in existence. The sourwoods are also of unusual size. These trees seldom attain a height of more than forty feet, and usually have to "lean" toward sunny spots beneath the bigger trees. Here they stand up boldly for their place in the sun.

CAROLINA HEMLOCK

It is interesting to note the size of the rhododendron leaves. Those forming the luxuriant forest understory along the trail are very large. Notice the difference when you come to the rim of the gorge. There the leaves are much tougher and smaller to withstand rugged weather.

SAND MYRTLE

The view of the lower falls will endure as a lifelong remembrance. You see a broad rock wall cleft by a narrow, twisted chasm through which the unseen water spirals down and then pours into view for the final plunge. The gray wall, some hundred and fifty feet across, is seamed with cracks. Carolina rhododendron, galax, and sand myrtle have somehow managed a toehold. Each spring, these and the Fraser magnolia of the lower slopes compose a "hanging gardens" older than Babylon.

Across the way is Long Arm Ridge, pinioned with dead trees. During the 1920s a fire seared the forest and glowered in the centuries-old duff, or humus, for weeks. "They fit that fire in there thirty days. I guess there are places in there now where you could fall down to your neck."

Long Arm is a spur from Jonas Ridge, the background mountain that "got hits name from a fellow named Jonas. Going from Morganton to Cranberry he got caught in a snow storm and froze to death."

The trail continues on to Erwins View, amid a heath garden along the rim of the gorge. The soil along the way is untypically sandy and explains the existence of an untypical plant, the turkey beard. It is one of the many species known as "bear grass." During midsummer it opens an attractive cluster of white blossoms, borne aloft on a single, leafless stalk.

Heath gardens are found throughout the mountains on rocky, exposed sites and are so named for the abundance of blossoming heaths that form them. Those found at Erwins View include the sand myrtle, blueberry, rhododendron, mountain laurel, leucothoe, and lyonia. The rare sweetleaf, or dye bush, is also abundant here.

Some folks use it to make yellow dye. The leaves are sweet and favored by "ole Dobbin."

The shrubs and surrounding trees are festooned with a pale green lichen known as cotton moss. It indicates that the local winds are full of moisture.

The view of Linville Gorge looks eastward, away from the falls into adjacent Pisgah National Forest. The shaggily timbered gorge is preserved as a wilderness area.

The view is always worth a last look. On the left the falls' constant roar becomes a kind of silence. The river through the gorge is a writhing whisper. Far below, a phoebe flutters out from a rock ledge, catches its insect prey, and returns to devour it. The river flows on. Thoughts are long, deep dreams.

Forest-Type Trees

eastern
  white pine
pitch or
  black pine
eastern hemlock
Carolina
  hemlock
Fraser
  magnolia
red maple
black or
  sour gum
sourwood
sassafras
serviceberry
white oak
chestnut oak
red oak
scarlet oak
black oak
chestnut sprouts
white ash
yellow poplar
  or tulip tree

black cherry
pin cherry
  (by rest rooms)
silky willow
flowering
  dogwood
flame azalea
swamp azalea
  (Upper Falls)
highbush
  blueberry
huckleberry
  (Erwins View)
rose acacia
  locust
  (Erwins View)
lyonia or
  maleberry
sweetleaf or
  dye bush
  (Erwins View)
chinquapin
  (Erwins View)
wild hydrangea
rosebay
  rhododendron

catawba
  rhododendron
Carolina
  rhododendron
mountain
  laurel
red-twig
  leucothoe
drooping
  leucothoe
  (Upper Falls)
cinnamonbush
witch hazel
withe-rod
  viburnum or
  shonny haw
  (Upper Falls)
ninebark
  (Upper Falls)
black
  chokeberry
  (Upper Falls)
yellowroot
  (Upper Falls)
spotted
  wintergreen

Common Ferns

New York fern
interrupted fern
Christmas fern

cinnamon fern
hay-scented
  fern

bracken
  (Erwins View)

Common Mosses

pin cushion
  moss or
  Leucobryum
green tussock
  moss or
  Dicranum

cotton moss
  (a "hanging"
  lichen)
fern moss or
  Thuidium

carpet moss or
  Hypnum
resurrection
  moss
  (a club moss)

Chestoa View Overlook

| **U.S. 221** | *Marion, 24 miles south; Asheville, 56 miles via U.S. 70 &* |
| **317.5 miles** | *I-40.* |

View of North Toe	*Gulf of Mexico drainage.*		
River Valley	*chestnut oak*	*cucumber tree*	*rosebay*
318.4 miles	*white oak*	*red maple*	*rhododendron*
elev. 3,540	*black oak*	*black locust*	*pignut hickory*

The North Toe River forms on Roan Mountain, close to the Tennessee border, and swings southwest alongside the Blue Ridge in a giant fishhook. Below, the infant river meanders over its broad valley toward the Black Mountains on the far horizon. Near the foot of this big range it joins the South Toe and flows eastward into Tennessee.

Toe is a contraction of the Cherokee "Estatoe," the name of a large Indian village in South Carolina. A well traveled trading path, the Estatoe Trail, led between the town and the Toe River region. Various tribes came great distances to dig for mica. They cut the glossy, sheetlike mineral into ornaments and sprinkled the glistening dust on the graves of their departed ones.

The Toe River region, referred to generally as the Spruce Pine District, is two hundred and fifty square miles of mineral wealth. Pegmatite, the native rock, contains large amounts of almost pure mica, feldspar, kaolin, and quartz. The excavations and pits of several mines are seen in the valley.

The conspicuously light-colored excavation in the foreground is a kaolin mine. The product is formed from leached feldspar and is used in the manufacture of high grade china. Exhibits of these and other minerals are shown in the Museum of North Carolina Minerals at Gillespie Gap, mile 331.

Humpback	The Parkway travels for over four miles along the mountain's upper slopes. Humpback has a feature not readily
Mountain	
319.8 miles	

The Parkway travels for over four miles along the mountain's upper slopes. Humpback has a feature not readily apparent. Viewed from a distance, it is an elongate dome with three knobs rising along its humped outline. The sides are a steep jumble of cliffs and snags. However, the hardy traveler who scales the top is surprised by the fairly level expanse over the summit. In this regard, Humpback is similar to many mountains in the Southern Highlands. A few have up to five hundred acres of land suitable for farming on top. The problem is how to get to and from the "farm."

Chestoa View	*white oak*	*black locust*	*Carolina*
320.8 miles	*red oak*	*sourwood*	*rhododendron*
elev. 4,090	*black oak*	*Carolina*	*flame azalea*
	pignut hickory	*hemlock*	*flowering*
	chestnut	*rosebay*	*dogwood*
	sprouts	*rhododendron*	

List continues

mountain laurel	red-twig	withe-rod
highbush	leucothoe	viburnum or
blueberry	lyonia	shonny haw
minniebush	mountain	
	winterberry	

Chestoa View, named by the poet traveler "Chucky Joe," is derived from the Cherokee word for rabbit. It is probable that he chose the name because of its poetic sound and not because the site ever abounded with cotton-tails.

A short trail heads down a wooded slope of Humpback Mountain to a rock balcony shaded by Carolina hemlock. The perpendicular rock face below is trellised with Carolina rhododendron, the cliff dweller of its group.

COTTONTAIL

In the deep, below Chucky Joe's Chestoa View, U.S. 221 extends from the Parkway through North Cove. The primitive wilderness known as Linville Gorge stretches between the long parallels of Linville Mountain and Jonas Ridge directly beyond. The tip of Hawksbill and the flat, tilted summit of Table Rock show on the right. High on the left, lofty and majestic, is Grandfather Mountain.

Bear Den Overlook
323.1 miles
elev. 3,359

The overlook stands above a forested hollow, a natural amphitheatre for bird song. Day long, and particularly during the quiet time before twilight, the songs come sweet and clear: wood warbler, wood thrush, towhee, and catbird.

In the straightaway, Linville Mountain slopes into the base of North Cove. To the right, the Parkway runs a collar around Whitenin' Spur and traces the Blue Ridge rambling in humble contrast toward the Black Mountains, long and high on the western skyline.

BEAR CLAW MARKS

The black bear once denned on the actual site of the overlook. When hard pressed by hunters and hounds, the bear clambered among the inaccessible cliffs and ledges of Humpback Mountain. Hidden from the hunter, he batted back the hounds as they tried to dislodge him.

Since the advent of the Parkway, when it literally blasted its way through the rocky barricade, the bear can no longer claim Humpback Mountain as his craggy retreat, but the same effect is still achieved. All land administered by the National Park Service is a refuge for wildlife.

Jackson Gap
324.8 miles
elev. 2,900

The gap was known at the turn of the 1800s as "Siah," or "Sier," for Josiah (Josier) Wiseman who got the land by grant.

Sometime prior to the Civil War it became Jackson Gap after a family of blacks by that name who settled nearby.

They were called "free Negroes," a term applied to

former slaves given their freedom, and to "free issues," the children of slaves, declared to be free at birth.

View of Apple Orchards from Heffner Gap
326 miles
elev. 3,057

Linville Mountain, long and straight, completely encloses the view. On the left, Honeycutt Mountain gambols down to the base of North Cove, lying between the two elevations. Rock cuts on Honeycutt's lower slope outline a portion of the Clinchfield's track up the Blue Ridge.

Whitenin' Spur stands above on the near right. What is that odd, flat-topped mountain poking up over there on the left? Table Rock.

In early May, just before the dogwood whitens the forest edge, the apple blossoms of Skylark Orchard shower the hillsides with pink-white fragrance. Their gardenlike arrangement contrasts with the unpatterned loveliness of the native wild flowers.

APPLE BLOSSOM

After the honeybees feast, the fruits begin to develop and grow in such abundance that the branches often need support. Many varieties are grown, both early and late, for eating and cooking. Siberian crabs ripen in August, but the bumper crops of Stark's Delicious, Stayman Winesap, York Imperial, and others ripen in October.

A resourceful widow, Amanda Heffner, once lived in the gap. A daughter of the pioneer Josiah Wiseman, she knew from childhood how to make her own way. During the "pinched" times of the Civil War era she ran her farm and raised a sturdy family.

View into North Cove
327.3 miles
elev. 2,815

Pepper Creek Valley leads directly into the North Cove community, lying at the base of Linville Mountain. A cove is a descriptive term often applied to areas of relatively flat land surrounded by mountains. The North Cove is enclosed by Honeycutt Ridge in the foreground and Linville Mountain beyond.

The land has remarkable fertility, being underlaid predominantly by limestone, and produces good hay and corn crops. The corn is husked by machines in the fields and hauled a few miles south to Marion for sale to the produce mills.

SCARLET OAK

On the right side of Pepper Creek Valley, seen through a screen of scarlet oaks, an orchard of Skylark farms covers a flank of the Blue Ridge. The orchard outlines a carefully defined "thermal zone," a frost-free area typical of the slopes below the Parkway.

Each evening cool mountain air flows down into the valleys. It tends to pool up in the hollows at the bottom. Hunters have long been aware of this trait and prefer to make their camp part way up a mountain where the climate is most mild.

In spring and fall, during time of frosts, killing freezes occur on the crests of the mountains and in the basal lowlands, but very rarely along the slopes. The constant flow of air helps prevent the existing moisture from turning into frost.

This knowledge is of great importance to orchardists, for the apple trees bloom and form fruit during the critical frost season of early May.

McKinney Gap
327.5 miles
elev. 2,790

From *Anthology of Death,* a group of obituaries by Uncle Jake Carpenter (1833-1920):

Charles McKinney, age 72
dide may 10 1852
ware farmer live in blew rige
had 4 womin
cors marid to 1
live at McKiney Gap
all went to fields to work to mak grane
all went to the crib for corn
all to smok house for mete
he cild 75 to 80 hogs a yer
and wimin never had no words bout his havin so many wimin
if it ware thes times thar wold be hare puld
thar war 42 children belong to him
they all went to preachin together
nothin sed
he made brandy all his life
never had no foes
got alon fin with everybodi
I nod him

Charles McKinney had a separate cabin for each wife. The homestead stood close by the Parkway route, just below the gap. As the need arose, McKinney hitched up his ox wagon and drove to Marion to trade farm produce for the many items needed by so numerous a family. Folks say that when he bought shoes they filled the wagon bed.

The famed pioneer trace, the Yellow Mountain Road, crossed the Blue Ridge at or very near McKinney Gap. It is believed that this transmountain route between North Carolina and Tennessee was blazed by James Robertson, aided by information from Daniel Boone.

Robertson led a wagon train of twelve families from the vicinity of Raleigh, N. C., across the mountains to the present site of Elizabethton, Tenn. They were primarily a group of defeated rebels known as the Regulators who lost to the king's forces at the Battle of Alamance in 1771. Their ire had been provoked by harsh methods of taxation and they sought to regulate matters by force of arms. Failing in this and in danger of losing their lives, many fled westward into the mountains. They added their numbers to the recently formed pioneer outpost completely on its own in the Watauga Valley of Tennessee.

The portion of their route known as the Yellow Mountain Road came west from Morganton across the end of Linville mountain, followed the North Fork of the Catawba to Pepper Ridge, and then swung up the mountain through McKinney Gap into the valley of the North Toe River. It followed to the headwaters of this stream, crossing the state line over the Unaka Range between the Roan Mountain and the Yellow Mountain, and descended to the Watauga River and the pioneer rallying point of Sycamore Shoals.

The Wataugans were also known as the "backwater men," because they lived on land drained by streams running "back" to the Gulf of Mexico, rather than "forward" to the Atlantic.

In 1763 the Crown had decreed all backwater land preserved as Indian hunting grounds. The Crown could so order but the Crown could not enforce. The "backwater men" leased land from the Indians and formed their own local government. Royal decrees could term them squatters, but they resolved to stay.

Within a decade they spoke their defiance, riding back over the mountains to settle accounts with the Tories at Kings Mountain.

**View of
"The Loops"**
*328.6 miles
elev. 2,980*

Below the domestic forest of the Skylark apple orchard, lens-shaped rock cuts on Rocky Mountain outline the path of the Clinchfield Railroad, conqueror of the Appalachians. Steadily and with awesome strength the diesel units loop upward along the mountain slopes, mighty motors throbbing, pulling the produce of fields and factories.

Over 31.5 miles of track, through eighteen tunnels, they ascend the Blue Ridge, averaging less than fifty vertical feet to the mile. After one hour and twenty minutes of all-out effort the singing motors of the crack "97" pull its steel caravan over the hump at McKinney Gap.

Extending from Spartanburg, S.C., to Elkhorn, Ky., the Clinchfield is the only railway cutting directly through the entire southern Appalachians. It culminates the dream of railmen and statesmen for a direct route between the cotton of the South and coal mines of the Midwest.

John C. Calhoun advocated the general route in 1832 but the necessary organization and capital did not materialize until 1886. Then the titanic struggle with the mountains began. Financial failures and even bloodshed retarded progress, but the rails were finally laid over the Blue Ridge in 1909 and welded into a steel transmountain link between East and Midwest in 1915.

This is the saga of the Clinchfield, named for the Clinch River it borders in Tennessee, and for the fields of coal and cotton between.

Swafford Gap
329.4 miles
elev. 2,852

On his crest-top farm, Marcus Swafford (1856-1943) lived as a spectator during that struggle between men and mountains when steel drivers and pick-and-shovel crews worked and sweated to lay the Clinchfield over the Blue Ridge.

The workers were rough and ready, many having recently arrived from Italy. Sometimes misunderstandings flamed into violence between immigrants and natives on the work force. Asked by his neighbors if things ever got out of hand, Marcus replied, "Oh not hardly. I've never seen more than two dead at the same time."

A few dead chestnut trees on the knoll southwest of the gap are the forlorn remains of Mr. Swafford's chestnut orchard. In the mountains the term has generally applied to any concentration of wild chestnut trees on a man's land.

But his orchard was kept clean and well tended. The chestnuts spread out like giant apple trees, yielding Marcus bumper harvests.

The chestnut blight, reaching farther southward from New York, year by year, struck and withered the trees in 1930. But for the blight, orchards like Marcus Swafford's would be contributing their considerable share to the ever-expanding economy of the mountains. *(1957)*

View of Table Rock
329.7 miles
elev. 2,870
Roadside easel:
Table Rock
Mountain

Table Mountain pine
pitch or black pine

Virginia pine
yellow poplar or tulip tree
flowering dogwood

The overlook is a spot for lazy thoughts, with cloud-islands drifting overhead and a whispering forest-sea covering the hills. Sounds from far away come in remarkably clear as though it were their intention to zero in on the listener. The shouts of boys playing far below come springing to your ears. The yelp of hounds, the drumming of grouse, the frequent melody of song birds ride updrafts of wind and seem to bring you nearer to the far away.

Miles beyond the range of hearing is one of the Parkway's finest, if more distant, views of Table Rock, its tilted summit rising behind the remarkably long, level crest line of Linville Mountain. Both are composed largely of quartzite, a fine-grained, durable rock. The imposing stretch of Linville Mountain indicates the stubborn resistance quartzite puts up against the forces of erosion.

Rocky Mountain, sloping unevenly downward in the foreground, was, in all probability, once equal in prominence to Linville Mountain. But the hard gneiss of which it is composed is weak compared to quartzite. Linville will still be high and proud in the eons to come when time and the elements will have worn Rocky Mountain away.

Whitenin' Spur, the imposing high point on Rocky Mountain, proves the wisdom of not jumping at conclusions. After reading the glossary of mountain terms given us by Uncle Newt, one would believe that the names of Whitenin' Spur and Rocky Mountain should be exchanged.

Gillespie Gap
330.9 miles
elev. 2,819

Museum of North Carolina Minerals

Overpass N. C. 226. Marion, 14 miles south; Spruce Pine, 5 miles north:

The Museum of North Carolina Minerals at Gillespie Gap contains exhibits of representative native minerals, including mica, feldspar, kaolin, spodumene, pyrophyllite, and tungsten.

Mica, the "insinglass window" of the old-fashioned stove and of the "surrey with the fringe on top," is a sparkling, transparent mineral widely distributed in many kinds of rocks. Generally, it occurs in individual flakes but occasionally may be found in highly compressed masses known as "mica books." Mica has many uses, principally as insulation and as an ingredient by the paint and rubber industries.

Feldspar, or "spar," is a variously colored mineral of medium hardness that occurs in extensive areas within the Spruce Pine District. The abundance of local feldspar makes North Carolina the leading producer of this important mineral. Most of the local product is used in the manufacture of glass and porcelain.

Feldspar deposits near the surface tend to disintegrate from the action of underground water and to form kaolin and halloysite, fine, white clays in high demand for the manufacture of china and other ceramics.

Spodumene, tungsten, and pyrophyllite are found in other parts of North Carolina. The first mineral is an ore of lithium, the lightest known metallic element. Pyrophyllite is an extremely soft talclike substance used for such varied purposes as slate pencils and as a base for insecticides. Tungsten, an extremely heavy metal with the highest known melting point, 6,700°C. (67 times the heat required to boil water) was formerly acquired from China until the urgencies of World War II made it necessary to find a local source. The high melting point of tungsten enables its use in light bulb filaments and as steel alloy for high speed tools, armor, and projectiles.

Many precious and semiprecious stones are found in North Carolina, particularly in the mountain region. The museum contains showcases of ruby, emerald, golden beryl, garnet, amethyst, quartz crystal, sapphire, and aquamarine. Several native "gemsmiths," including Lee McKinney, Floyd Grant, and Floyd Wilson, have mastered the art of cutting and polishing the stones and fashioning them into exquisite jewelry.

All the gold rushes in America's romantic history did

Gillespie Gap Minerals Museum

not take place in the West of the Forty-niners, or the Alaskan Klondike. For many years, centering around 1833, North Carolina led the nation in gold production. Though mines were known to be in operation before the Revolution, the first recorded instance of a find was a whopping seventeen pound nugget discovered by two children, a brother and sister, in 1799.

The museum also contains view-box displays of weirdly glowing fluorescent minerals, and a selection of the rare, exceedingly heavy radioactive ores.

You will find that the museum portrays the various minerals in interesting and understandable terms. After your visit, minerals will be more than hunks of rock with odd sounding names. You will know them as valuable raw materials from which many of the familiar comforts and necessities of our way of life are obtained.

The Kings Mountain Men

On September 29, 1780, a grim troop of over 1,100 mounted men under the commands of John Sevier and Isaac Shelby passed southward through Gillespie Gap to search out and battle Ferguson and his Tories.

Major Patrick Ferguson, a Scotsman in the British army, roamed the piedmont at will, terrorizing the patriots and organizing Loyalist support. To the hostile backwater men he issued an ultimatum: if they did not desist from their opposition to British arms and take protection under his standard, he would march his army over the mountains, hang their leaders, and lay their country waste with fire and sword.

It was not an empty threat. General Charles Cornwallis, the commanding British officer in the South, occupied Charleston. In August his forces had routed the Americans at Camden. The Patriot cause looked bleak.

But the mountain men met the challenge, mustering a mounted infantry from Tennessee, Virginia, and the Carolinas. They were joined by other forces at the foot of the Blue Ridge, and tracked Ferguson to Kings Mountain in northwestern South Carolina.

The night of September 29 a portion of the force camped below the Blue Ridge at Henry Gillespie's, a hardy Irishman who had been, perhaps, a dozen years in the country, and from whom the neighboring gap took its name. Whatever Gillespie's sympathies may have been, he remained a determined neutral so as to protect his family from the Indian allies of the British. As a precautionary measure the mountaineers kept him in camp overnight, but released him the following morning.

After a week's march this frontier army under the command of Col. William Campbell of Virginia located Ferguson at Kings Mountain. With a picked force of 910, they moved on Ferguson's combat-ready force of 1,125 American Tories.

The sharp, decisive battle destroyed Ferguson and started a chain reaction that led to the capitulation of Cornwallis at Yorktown a year later. A few of the mountain men were present at the surrender, but most hastened home to fight the threatening Cherokee. In whirlwind skirmishes they reaffirmed their conquest of the red men.

Penland School of Handicrafts

Penland, 12 miles north on N.C. 226, is the home of Penland School of Handicrafts, a Shangri-la in the mountains inhabited by charming handicrafters from the Southern Highlands and all the wide world. Handicrafters are sublimely contented people who do creative things with their hands and minds: weaving, pottery, metal crafts, ceramics, leather work, spinning, painting, and playing shepherds' pipes.

Lynn Gap
332.6 miles
elev. 3,109

BASSWOOD OR LYNN

Once an ancient lynn, known as the "marrying tree," spread its shade over Lynn Gap. When young lovers of the mountainous country of Mitchell found true love blighted by an unrelenting parent or some other unromantic pitfall, like as not they'd hie to the marrying tree.

But it had to be done in an "unbeknownst" fashion. The aspiring groom-to-be enlisted a trusted friend to journey in secret down mountain to the county of McDowell, there to find a preacher.

After proper persuasion, up-saddled the preacher and off the two headed for the county line. Waiting for them, anxious and eager, was the lovey-dovey pair. Close by the dividing line stood a tremendous lynn. What better place to be married than beneath its shading boughs.

Thusly were they and others wed. And a legend came to pass that whomsoever wedded beneath the tree were destined to stay that way. When a pair went to all that trouble to tie the knot, it would never unravel:

"Whomsoever weds beneath my boughs
Shall ever keep their marriage vows."

The lynn, linden, or basswood, though not a common tree, is widely distributed in the highlands, particularly on moist slopes.

The small, cream-colored flowers open in June. They are fragrant and honey-rich, and along with sourwood are one of the "bee trees."

To Uncle Newt the wood is "soft as pine, easy broke, and not very stout. Hits a good, smooth lumber, easy worked. Not many knots. A 'particular' man might take hit fur makin' his ceilin'."

The name of lynn comes from Europe where others of this genus are also found. The strong inner bark, once used as cordage, was known as "linde." In early America the inner bark served the same purpose but was referred to as "bass" or "bast."

The **Little Switzerland Tunnel** is 575 feet long.
333.4 miles.

Little Switzerland
333.9 miles
elev. 3,490
N.C. 226A
Parkway exit

Here on the southeastern edge of the Carolina mountains, Little Switzerland overlooks the green tumble of foothills and spurs that stretches from the Blue Ridge like the wings of an albatross.

While conversing with a companion who had recently been to Switzerland, Judge Heriot Clarkson was told how the scenery for his summer home resembled the Swiss Jura Mountains, a green rolling land along the French border. From this friendly conversation the name of Little Switzerland evolved.

Bearwallow Gap
335.4 miles
elev. 3,482

On hot days or nights, the black bear enjoys the pig-like pleasure of wallowing in the cold muck about springs. He will roll and root through the ooze, wonderfully content to be free from heat and flies.

The frequent occurrence of springs in low places along the mountain crest line accounts for the numerous ''Bearwallow Gaps.'' This one is nearby on the western side of the motor road. Another Bearwallow Gap is located along the Parkway in Virginia at Mile 91.

Gooch Gap
336.3 miles
elev. 3,360

''Really is Coots Gap. On some old land papers of mine it calls fur a 'tree in Coots Gap.' Coots was said to be a hunter. He had a camp built over there.

''This was way before my time. Back when I was a young feller them government men makin' map surveys come through askin' people the names of places. I remember talkin' to one of 'm. He was ridin' an old mule.

''The best I can figure is he didn't hear the name right.''
(Reid Queen, Little Switzerland, N.C., (1955)

Gooch is an English name of early record. The first Gooches in the Carolina mountains came about the time of the Revolution and were said to be Tories. Their neighbors evidently pronounced ''Gooch'' as ''Gouge,'' for so they are known today.

Wildacres Tunnel
336.8 miles
313 feet long

The ridge through which the tunnel passes dips sharply, then builds abruptly into a forested knob about eye level with the Parkway. A group of buildings are clustered on top, ''hanging by their eyebrows.'' This is Wildacres, the dream project of Thomas Dixon, 1864-1946, an impassioned champion of the Old South and prolific author. Two of his most popular works are *The Leopard's Spots*, and *The Clansman*, better known under its movie title, *Birth of a Nation*.

Dixon bought the land in 1921 to develop into a scenic retreat. Authors were invited to take up residence among the wild but inspiring mountain acres.

The venture fared well for a time but shared a common downfall with enterprise in general during the 1929 crash. Since that time, Wildacres has been occupied by an artist colony and is now a Chatauqua-type conference center.

**View from
Deerlick Gap**
*337.2 miles
elev. 3,452
Roadside easel:
Woodchucks.
Two-mile trail to
Three Knobs
Overlook.*

*scarlet oak
white oak
black oak
white ash
sweet or
     black birch
mockernut
     hickory*

*pignut hickory
red maple
pitch or
     black pine
sourwood
black locust
flowering
     dogwood*

*sassafras
yellow poplar
     or tulip tree
serviceberry
dwarf sumac*

On the left, Lake James is a far off bit of blue in the Catawba Valley, seen beyond the gradual decline of Linville Mountain. The long stretch of Wood Mountain dominates the foreground.

Certain rocks in Deerlick Gap are said to contain saltpeter. Deer will travel many miles for salt, not only the table variety, but various other mineral salts as well. Early hunters, including, perhaps, the forgotten Mr. Coots of Gooch Gap, hid by the deerlick in quest of venison.

**View from
Three Knobs**
*338.8 miles
elev. 3,880*

Seven Mile Ridge slopes away like a crooked finger between the Parkway and the ponderous outline of the Black Mountains. It separates the South Toe River Valley beyond from the quiet glen drained by Crabtree Creek below.

An old sled road extends along the crest of Seven Mile Ridge from Crabtree Meadows to the small trading center of Newdale on the South Toe. Parts of the road are still used by farmers, walking beside or leisurely riding their horse-drawn sleds.

The early mountain roads often followed a ridge instead of a river valley. A water course frequently led to a dead end against the mountains. Many long spurs, or ridges like Seven Mile Ridge, have a fairly even crest line and are more directional than the meanderings of a stream.

The view from the overlook is one of many on the Parkway deservingly described as spectacular. But it hits the zenith in October. The forests become a vast, lavish mosaic of gilded color.

**Crabtree Meadows
Recreation Area**
*339.5 miles
253 acres*

Naturalist program: amphitheatre, nature walks; hiking trails; picnic grounds; campgrounds; trailer camp; rest rooms; coffee shop; gift shop; service station.

The meadows and adjoining forest are a cool and delightful summer retreat, almost within the shadow of the massive Black Mountains range. Each May the

Crabtree Falls

flowering crab becomes pink with blossoms, highlighting a colorful wildflower display. Through the picnic grounds and the trails leading into forested hollow, May is tinted with crested dwarf iris, columbine, lady's slipper, and showy orchids. June follows with speckled wood lily, goatsbeard, sundrop, beard tongue, and mountain laurel. The display continues into summer and fall with rosebay rhododendron, wave aster, white snakeroot, and gentian.

The white snakeroot, showy though it may be, was probably an unsuspected source of trouble to the early settlers of the meadows. Particularly during dry weather when pasture is scarce, cattle sometimes eat the plant and thereby poison their milk. Years ago, this was known as the "milk-sick," a little understood but frequently fatal malady. People with a reputation for curing it were known as "milk-sick" doctors. The most effective remedy is still hot sugar, whiskey, and plenty of rest. Local veterinarians use the same treatment for Bossy when she eats the weed and "comes down with the trembles."

The early settlers knew this area as the Blue Ridge Meadows, a name of such vintage that it is possible the meadows were fire-cleared by the Indians. The Penland family acquired the land in a grant from the king, but it was probably not settled until well after the Revolution.

During the early 1800s, through the Civil War, hard-working Billy Bradshaw ran the property for the Penlands. Billy, in turn, hired several families to help tend the livestock and grow crops.

But he did every bit of his share. A chief occupation was the operation of a corn mill on the upper reaches of Crabtree Creek. Folks from South Toe River Valley and all along the Seven Mile Ridge brought their "turns" of corn up to Billy Bradshaw's mill.

Unlike the Parkway's well known Mabry Mill, Bradshaw's did not have an overshot wheel turned by water pouring over it. Billy had a "tub," or turbine mill. The mill wheel lay horizontally at stream-bed level and was turned by water flowing through a trough and striking it at a downward angle. This type mill was especially adapted to mountain streams, with their rapid but small rate of flow.

There are many place-names within the meadows area to recall Billy Bradshaw's time, but most remain in name only. The picnic grounds are in the "loggy patch." When Bradshaw first began to clear the land, he deadened the timber by girdling the trees. Crops were then raised beneath the leafless stand.

Customarily the trees were later cut down and hauled off and burned. But this particular "dead'nin'" got out of hand. It grew into a "loggy patch" of windblown trees and sprouting undergrowth, much more suited to foraging cattle than crop raising. Oftentimes, when a farmer set out to hunt a stray cow, he was told by a neighbor, "Las' time

FLOWERING CRAB

WHITE SNAKEROOT

I seen your cattle, it was over by the loggy patch.'' And so the name stuck. Nearby are the "wheat patch," the "rye patch," and the "nettle patch."

About two miles south on the Parkway, close to the motor road, is the site of the Last Chance Baptist Church. It served as a place of worship and learning for the people of Blue Ridge Meadows during the generation after Billy Bradshaw.

Built in the first decade of the 1900s, the church stood for over twenty years, "way up thar" in the mountains. It was a man's last chance for religion. If he didn't get it here, he wouldn't find it any farther on.

For two or three of the winter months school was held in the church, presided over by a state school teacher, one of the first in the mountain country. The pupils sat on split-log benches during the process of absorbing their readin', 'ritin', and 'rithmetic. At noon recess the boys and girls gathered in separate groups to play games. Tag ball was a great young fellers' favorite. The "it" boy tried to tag one of the other players by hitting him with the ball. A particular pleasure was to "set his britches a-fire" with a well-aimed throw. The girls delighted in skipping rope, the rope consisting of a long grapevine.

Just before and during the twenties, the young people began to drift away from the meadows, lured into the industrial valleys by jobs in textile mills and factories. The old folks stayed on, mostly 'til they passed away.

Now the beautiful uplands are a recreational area of the Parkway, snugly set within the Pisgah National Forest. In common with Doughton Park, Peaks of Otter, and other like areas it is an invitation to stay awhile and get acquainted. Its feature attraction is Crabtree Falls.

A path from the picnic grounds weaves downward to it through a hollow. As you walk along, the ever present wind sends a soft, rushing sound through the leaves. Unnoticed, another sound much like that of wind and leaves blends in. It grows and grows. You suddenly realize it is the falls. The path leads on toward the sound through a leaning overhead of birch and hemlock. And then you see the falls, a downward dance of spray and mist. And you feel wonderful.

CHIPMUNK

Parkway Guide *continues*

Forest Trees and Shrubs

Oak-hickory with a great variety of other broadleaf trees, over a dogwood, a rosebay rhododendron, mountain laurel, flame azalea understory. Very few conifers other than a fair amount of hemlock.

red oak
white oak
chestnut oak
scarlet oak
black oak
mockernut hickory
pignut hickory
sweet or black birch
yellow birch
yellow poplar or tulip tree
flowering dogwood
rosebay rhododendron
mountain laurel
flame azalea
hop-hornbeam
mountain winterberry
witch hazel

flowering crab
red maple
striped maple
sugar maple
chestnut sprouts
black or sour gum
pin or fire cherry
serviceberry
sourwood
white ash
minniebush
highbush blueberry
oil nut
sassafras
withe-rod or shonny haw viburnum
mapleleaf viburnum
red-twig leucothoe

drooping leucothoe
butternut
Fraser magnolia
cucumber tree
basswood
beech
yellow buckeye
eastern hemlock
Carolina hemlock
eastern white pine
pitch or black pine
cinnamonbush
American elder
hawthorn
beaked filbert
winged sumac
smooth sumac
wild grape
greenbriar

TOWHEE

BROWN THRASHER

Ground flowers

Spring

violet
buttercup
toothwort
lousewort
Robin's plantain
yellow lady's slipper
showy orchid

columbine
painted trillium
large-flowered trillium
may apple
geranium
field hawkweed
golden ragwort

small's ragwort
trailing arbutus
wild ginger
foamflower
blue cohosh
wild sarsaparilla
fire pink

Summer

solomon's seal
solomon's plume
uvularia
speckled wood lily
galax
goatsbeard

spiderwort
beard tongue
alumroot
early meadow rue
dutchman's pipe
purple flowering raspberry

crow poison
wild hydrangea
small-flowered bunchflower
bowman's root
black snakeroot

Late Summer

wild licorice
tall bellflower
orange hawkweed

golden aster
Indian plantain
Joe-pye weed

spotted touch-me-not
pale touch-me-not

Autumn

great lobelia	heath aster	wrinkled goldenrod
white wood aster	white snakeroot	bull thistle
bigleaf aster	curtis goldenrod	bottle gentian
swamp aster	tall goldenrod	

Ferns (most along trail to falls)

INTERRUPTED FERN

cinnamon fern	hay-scented fern	shield fern
interrupted fern	polypody fern	marginal shield fern
broad beech fern	Christmas fern	bracken
lady fern	maiden-hair fern	
	New York fern	

Birds and other Wildlife

raven	goldfinch	yellow-throat
crow	indigo bunting	black-throated blue warbler
bluejay	towhee	chestnut-sided warbler
crested flycatcher	grasshopper sparrow	black-and-white warbler
wood peewee	field sparrow	hooded warbler
phoebe	chipping sparrow	prairie warbler
downy woodpecker	song sparrow	southern parula warbler
flicker	cardinal	cedar waxwing
bluebird	scarlet tanager	mourning dove
robin	red-eyed vireo	ruffed grouse
wood thrush	blue-headed vireo	bobwhite
meadowlark	white-breasted nuthatch	turkey vulture
Carolina wren	ruby-throated hummingbird	gray squirrel
catbird	ovenbird	chipmunk
brown thrasher	Louisiana water thrush	fencepost lizard
black-capped chickadee		
Carolina junco		

View of Black Mountain Range
342.2 miles
elev. 3,892
Roadside easel: The Black Mountains

The Black Mountain range is a "motif" of western grandeur. Big and bold, it rises up to the clouds. The individual peaks are not conspicuous. It is the range that dominates the horizon. A dark green mane of red spruce and Fraser fir covers the crest and gives reason for the name of Black Mountains.

These are the highest mountains in the East, with an average elevation exceeding 6,000 feet and towering 4,000 feet above the basal lowlands. The Canadian type climate seldom exceeds temperatures in the 70s during summer and has dropped to 23 below zero in winter. The rainfall averages more than 70 inches annually with a recorded maximum of 108, second on this continent only to the rain forests of the Pacific Northwest.

Within the Blacks dwell many of the birds familiar to far northern forests: Canada warbler, brown creeper, rose-breasted grosbeak, red-breasted nuthatch, and the winter wren. To the nature lover it would be worth a climb up the mountain to hear the winter wren's exuberant melody or the rich carol of the grosbeak. No one need be so energetic, however. The thin line ascending the Blacks represents a state highway from the Parkway to the summit.

The Black Mountains, like the surrounding ranges, are composed of a hard gneiss consisting primarily of quartz, feldspar, mica, and hornblende. The Blacks probably contain a higher percentage of quartz. The extreme durability of this mineral would cause a greater resistance to erosion and so helps explain the superior height of the range.

WHITE-TAILED DEER

Some fifteen million years ago the Appalachian mountain system underwent an extensive uplift. The entire region was gradually shoved upward several thousand feet. It is thought that the Blacks received a proportionately high degree of uplift, which would further account for their great height.

The entire range is in the form of a fishhook. The curved end butts against the Parkway, miles 355-360. The view from this overlook is of the eastern and highest arm. The short western arm forms the background view from Craggy Dome overlook, mile 364.

Buck Creek Gap
344.1 miles
elev. 3,373

Overpass N.C. 80; Marion, 16 miles southeast; Burnsville, 18 miles northwest.

The name "buck" refers to the presence of deer, once abundant, then diminished, and now abundant again in response to successful game management.

Buck Creek, Atlantic drainage, heads at the gap and flows southeast past Singecat Ridge into Lake Tahoma and the Catawba River.

The South Toe River, Gulf of Mexico drainage, accepts Three Forks Creek descending on the other side (trout streams).

In 1831 a meeting known as the Esteville Convention was held in Virginia to discuss construction of a wagon toll from Ohio through Kentucky and Tennessee into North Carolina. Crossings were investigated at McKinney Gap, Turkey Cove (Gillespie) Gap, and Buck Creek Gap.

Although the project never got beyond the reconnaissance stage, it points up the urgent need of that time for good transmountain routes. The Appalachians cut the country in half, hampering commerce and isolating the mountain region from the flow of national life.

This isolation is now all but dissolved by the energetic and continuing road program of recent years.

Twin Tunnels	344.5 miles	344.7 miles
	North Tunnel	South Tunnel
	294 feet	407 feet

**Singecat Ridge
Overlook**
*345.3 miles
elev. 3,406*

Snub-nosed Onion Knob on the left, and the big ramble of Mackey Mountain on the right, funnel the view into Lake Tahoma, a blue reservoir on Buck Creek.

Singecat Ridge lies out of view behind Onion Knob. The name implies that someone's house cat got barbered by a fire of some sort, but not even Uncle Newt ever "heard tell of how hit got its name."

The ridge came to grief during a fire in the spring of 1955 and was thoroughly singed. New green has finally covered its desolate nakedness.

Onion Knob, where a sharp flavored type of "wet weather" onion grows each spring, shows an interesting tilted wall of bare rock. The wall is the remnant of a series of *U*-shaped rock folds and illustrates the underlying reason for the formation of many mountain valleys.

The slope guided the direction of streams which, in turn, gradually enlarged a passageway along the bottom of the *U*.

Big Laurel Gap
*347.6 miles
elev. 4,048*

U.S. Forest Service Road: northwest to Black Mountain campgrounds.

Laurel is the name throughout the Parkway region for rhododendron, and "big" laurel signifies the *Rhododendron maximum,* or rosebay. In favorable locations it attains a height of thirty to forty feet. Reputedly a very large specimen once stood in the gap, along a mountain footpath.

The forest understory on this stretch of Parkway between Buck Creek Gap and Ridge Junction, miles 344-355, is predominantly a glossy evergreen of rosebay and of catawba rhododendron. They are the common native species.

LEAF OF ROSEBAY AND CATAWBA
RHODODENDRON

When in bloom, lavish purple identifies the catawba, and shell-pink blossoms set forth the rosebay. At other times they are hard to distinguish. From the roadside, each is a dark green cluster of leathery leaves. Those of the rosebay are noticeably tapered and more narrow. The catawba's leaves are more rounded at the tip and have silvery undersides.

The positive way of distinguishing catawba is by the bloom buds forming for the coming year. Each bud is prominent and plump, covered with broad, snugly compressed scales. The rosebays differ in having a conspicuous basal ring of loose, narrow scales.

In general the rosebay grows in more sheltered locations, whereas its purple-flowering counterpart thrives in rocky, exposed sites. In places where both can adapt, it's mainly a case of "whichever gits thar fustest."

The service road of the Pisgah National Forest leads a few miles northwest to a well-stocked fishing paradise on Neal Creek. Big, pampered trout rise willingly to the fly. No male anglers need make the trip, however, for the fishing is restricted to women and children.

**Rough Ridge
Tunnel**
*349 miles
245 feet*

Tunnels are used as nesting sites by rough-winged swallows.

**View from Head
of Licklog Ridge**
*349.2 miles
elev. 4,602*

Table Mountain pine to the left of the overlook sign, pitch or black pine to the right.

A clear day view from the overlook is one of the Parkway's best. When the mist is not too much with us, Grandfather Mountain noses skyward on the far left. Extending forward, away from the Blue Ridge, is long, long Linville Mountain with profiles of Hawksbill and flat-topped Table Rock appearing to be part of Linville's crest line.

The sinuous surge of Wood Mountain, lies in the middle distance on the left.

In the outlying flatlands, blue islands identify visible portions of Lake James in the Catawba Valley. Long, low, and mistily vague, the South Mountains lie on the far side of the valley. In the evening, clusters of lights locate the town of Marion.

Directly in front, left to right, rise the twin domes of Mackey Mountain and Chestnut Wood Mountain. Several generations ago a native had a private lead mine somewhere in that mountainous maze and made his own bullets.

Every now and then a rumor of its being found makes the embers of interest glow brightly.

"Hit's not no rumor, buddy, and I just might know where it's at." "Where is it?" "I'm not a-tellin'." So.

Curtis Creek flows directly below past the right side of Chestnut Wood Mountain and into the upper Catawba Valley. The Hickory Nut Mountains form the background for this forest-green ramble of hills.

On the near right a steep ridge pokes up abruptly to form the nasal profile of Snook's Nose. Beyond the Snook, the Blue Ridge leaves a winglike wake of mighty spurs as it roams off on the far right into the shaggy loveliness of the Lake Lure country.

For more than a century before the government began,

about 1913, acquiring the rough land below for the Pisgah National Forest, herds of cattle, horses, sheep, and swine lived off the wilderness land. For a number of years thereafter, the National Forest maintained a fenced range of twenty-seven thousand acres covering both sides of the Blue Ridge. Farmers paid $.90 a head for the right to graze their cattle spring through fall. In 1927 the new highway over Buck Creek Gap made it impossible to gate the fence properly and the practice was discontinued.

During the grazing seasons herders made occasional trips to the animals to keep them "tame" and provide them with salt. Generally, salt was poured into a row of holes chopped out of a large log or fallen tree. The licklog lay by a spring or other site where animals came.

BLACKBEAR

Licklog Ridge steeps abruptly downward on the right. Directly below, at the head of Curtis Creek, is the plunging Bear Drive Branch.

To the mountain herders bears were hated predators. The men could not stay with the livestock for constant protection, but they hunted and trapped bear at every opportunity.

If a bear became too destructive, the local people joined in a drive, turning all their dogs loose on the hot trail of the bold cattle killer. The hunted bear might run and fight all day, but sooner or later he ran for rugged country like that seen directly below, and stood at bay there against the pursuing dogs.

PANTHER

Several hunters, who had posted themselves at good vantage points, or "bear stands," waited for a chance to make the kill.

The mountain men waged successful war on all large predators. Their guns exterminated the panther before the turn of the century, though reports persist of a remnant few. Wolves lingered into the second decade. Bears almost disappeared over most of their range by the 1920s. But, with recognition of game as a resource, their numbers have increased considerably.

Annual hunts hold their numbers in check. The bear keeps to the forest and leaves mankind and his possessions alone.

View of Mount Mitchell
349.9 miles
elev. 4,821
Roadside easel: the story of a tragedy

The broad central dome of the Black Mountains crest line identifies 6,684-foot Mount Mitchell, highest in eastern America. On the left, two mastlike antennae of a radio station mark Clingman's Peak, 6,567 feet. These two eminences rise in mute testimony to a tragedy in the ways of men and mountains.

In 1824 Dr. Elisha Mitchell, a native of Connecticut, came to the University of North Carolina as a professor of sciences. From the famed French botanist, André Michaux, he heard of the mighty Blacks and first visited them in 1835. By means of barometer readings on several of the high points he determined that the Blacks, rather

Mount Mitchell

than Mt. Washington of New Hampshire, represented the top elevation in the East.

Again in 1844 Mitchell returned to make further and more precise measurements. He enlisted the aid of Big Tom Wilson, a bear hunter and guide who knew the country like the back of his hand.

The same year, Thomas L. Clingman, statesman, soldier, and ardent mountaineer, measured several of the Black Mountain peaks. In a published account of his observations he claimed to have found a peak higher than the one measured by Dr. Mitchell. A scholarly dispute developed between the two scientists, enlivening the lecture hall and the pages of newsprint and journals. Both gentlemen agreed that Clingman had measured the highest point. The unsettled question was whether or not Dr. Mitchell had done so previously.

In 1857 Mitchell completed plans to revisit the mountains and settle the issue. He commenced in a thorough manner, making a series of measurements from Morganton below the mountains in the east, to a place on the Blue Ridge appropriately known as the halfway house. From here he set out alone for the home of Big Tom to enlist his aid as a guide.

The mountains were shrouded in fog and the footing treacherous over the damp rocks and underbrush. Darkness came with unforeseen suddenness. Mitchell, feeling his way along a bear trail, lost his balance and plunged to his death over a waterfall. For more than a week a large number of searchers covered the rough forests. Their anxious concern turned to gloomy resignation. They now hoped at least to find the body and give it a Christian burial.

When the news reached Big Tom in his remote cabin at the foot of the Blacks, he turned to his wife and grimly remarked, ''Mother, that poor man's dead up there on the mountain.'' Wilson figured that the professor had been on the way to his house over a path known to both of them. Carefully he searched for the faded evidence of Mitchell's route and by following telltale signs in the underbrush and along the ground he picked up the trail. It led to the place now known as Mitchell's Falls on the north side of the Blacks, and to recovery of the body.

Thomas Clingman surrendered his claim. Dr. Mitchell lies enshrined in a granite grave atop the high peak.

While it is fully conceded that the name of Dr. Mitchell rests deservedly on the high peak, it is doubtful that he ever measured it as such. He apparently accorded the honor to a slightly lower peak formerly known as Mt. Mitchell.

The controversy, insofar as it involved Clingman, was of a highly personal nature. An ambitious man, Clingman had powerful rivals who adopted the cause of the scholarly Mitchell. Clingman claimed that he climbed the mountain then known as Mt. Mitchell and sighted measurements on Big Black, a high domed summit to the north. This he found to be higher than any eastern peak previously measured, and published his claim.

Big Black is now known as Mt. Mitchell. The former Mt. Mitchell is now called Clingman's Peak. The second elevation to the right of Mt. Mitchell bears the name of Big Tom, best guide and bear hunter the Black Mountains ever knew.

**View from
Green Knob**
*350.4 miles
elev. 4,761*

Green Knob (elev. 4,950) humps behind the overlook. In long ago days the knob was burned over and the second growth sprouts of the following years leafed out sooner than in the surrounding forest and made the mountain conspicuously green.

The view looks into the headwaters region of the Catawba River, once the homeland of the Catawba Indians. Beyond the valley rise the low and compact Hickory Nut Mountains. To the right, row upon row of long spurs descend from the Blue Ridge as it roams casually away from the Parkway at Ridge Junction.

The Catawba Indians, according to tribal tradition, came to this country as nomad buffalo hunters from the northwest. Finding the land to their liking, they stayed on and became a nation of farmers as well as hunters.

The Catawba are believed to be an eastern branch of the great Siouan stock that includes Dakota, Iowa, Crow, and Sioux.

Catawba territory followed southeast below the Blue Ridge along the big river bearing their name, into South Carolina. Juan Pardo, the resolute lieutenant of DeSoto, passed through their homeland in 1560 and about a hundred years later the Catawba played host to John Lederer, the wide-ranging agent of Virginia's governor Sir William Berkeley.

During these years the Catawba numbered an estimated 5,000 people, but wars with the Cherokee, Iroquois, and whites reduced them to nearly a fourth that number by 1721. From this time on the Catawba allied themselves with the white man and a fate of gradual decline. A few hundred live today at Sugar Creek, S.C.

Catawba folklore lives more permanently than the tribe. A tale that held young braves-to-be into crouched statues of attention told of a great battle on Roan Mountain, 'way across the Blue Ridge above the Tennessee Valley. The Catawba accepted the challenge of all other nations in the world and fought three battles on the broad mountain top. Blood ran freely but the Catawba conquered.

Three "heath balds," like those at Craggy Gardens, covered with catawba rhododendron, mark the battle grounds. Each June they bloom red from the blood of the Catawba and their foes.

Deep Gap
351.9 miles
elev. 4,284

U.S. Forest Service Road to Black Mountain Campgrounds

Deep Gap is a descriptive name of frequent repetition. Three lie across the crest line route of the Parkway and a fourth is seen on the profile of the Black Mountains.

The Pinnacle
354 miles
elev. 5,666

The mountain summit opposite the milepost on the southeast marks the point where the Parkway leaves the Blue Ridge and passes along a short connecting ridge to the Black Mountains. Surpassed only by Grandfather Mountain, 5,938 feet, the pinnacle is the second highest in the entire Blue Ridge from Pennsylvania to Georgia. It marks the southern limit of the Parkway's location along the drainage divide between the Atlantic slope and the Gulf of Mexico.

The Parkway enters onto the divide in Floyd County, Virginia, near mile 140, and follows it a total distance of 214 road miles. North from Floyd County all the streams flowing from the Parkway region enter the Atlantic. South of the pinnacle, the Parkway travels over mountains whose streams enter the Gulf.

Black Mountain Gap
355.3 miles
elev. 5,160

Black Mountain Gap was formerly called Swannanoa Gap, as it is located above the headwaters of the Swannanoa River. Map makers made the change to prevent confusion with the well known Blue Ridge gap of the same name, marking the Blue Ridge crossing of Interstate Highway 40 between Old Fort and Black Mountain, N.C.

At this location a logging railway came up to the Blue Ridge from Black Mountain, crossed onto the Black Range, and carried up into the high spruce forests. The modern state highway, N.C. 128, slanting upward from the Parkway to Mt. Mitchell State Park, follows the general route of the railway and of the Perley-Crockett auto toll road that operated afterward until 1939.

View from Ridge Junction
355.4 miles
elev. 5,160

4.8 miles to Mt. Mitchell State Park on N.C. 128.

The foreground forest, from the spruce-trimmed crest line of the Blacks to the hemlock bottoms of the South Toe Valley, comprises about half of the 32,000-acre Mt. Mitchell Cooperative Management Area.

Within this domain, managed jointly by the Pisgah National Forest and the North Carolina Wildlife Resources Commission, practices are applied to encourage the production of game.

Game technicians make clearings in the forest to increase the amount of "edge," or forest border, where plant and insect food is most plentiful. An occasional "den tree" with a hollow trunk is preserved for squirrels or the locally rare raccoon and opossum. Saplings and rhododendron are slashed in winter for deer browse.

CANADA WARBLER

In management areas, game is a crop harvested each year. This particular crop consists of deer, bear, grouse, rabbit, and gray squirrel. Hunters come each fall and winter to test their skill against the mountains and the quarry.

Mount Mitchell State Park
4.8 miles on N.C. 128

Nature museum and trails; picnic and campgrounds (tents only); restaurant.

Whenever the swelter of summer is upon you, here is a place to "take the time and stay awhile," at least half a day. Though heat waves shimmer in the lowlands far below, here it is cool and breezy on the sunniest day.

Picnickers should bring a sweater and campers an extra blanket.

A natural history museum tells you about the plant and animal life of this northern haunt. Nature trails lead through the moist, mossy forests of spruce and balsam.

The observation tower on the crest of Mount Mitchell, 6,684 feet, is the highest place in eastern America. Nearby is the grave of Dr. Elisha Mitchell for whom the mountain is named. The grave marker reads:

RUFFED GROUSE

> Here lies in the hope of a blessed resurrection the body of Rev. Elisha Mitchell, D.D., who, after being for 39 years a professor in the University of North Carolina, lost his life in the scientific exploration of this mountain in the sixty-fourth year of his age, June 27th, 1857.

Asheville Watershed
355.4-366.0 miles

Over a distance of fifteen miles, the Parkway passes through several sections of the Asheville watershed. This 20,000-acre area is on the slopes of the Blue Ridge, Black, and Great Craggy Mountains. Clear mountain streams pour into reservoirs for the city of Asheville and its vicinity.

The blue of North Fork reservoir sparkles below the Parkway at the foot of the Great Craggies.

The watershed contains one of the few remaining virgin spruce-fir forests in the Southeast. Between Ridge Junction and Balsam Gap, a distance of 4.5 miles, the Parkway travels through a resinous, deep green glimpse of the Canadian North.

Blackstock Knob
358 miles elev. 6,325

Blackstock Knob domes above the Parkway. Located on the bend of the "fishhook" Blacks, it is the highest point on the short, western arm. Nemiah Blackstock, for whom the mountain is named, surveyed the surrounding terrain in 1845.

Highest point on the Parkway north of Asheville, 5,676 feet, is at mile 358.5.

*red spruce
Fraser balsam
or fir
beech*

*yellow buckeye
yellow birch
mountain maple
red elder*

Balsam Gap marks the junction of the Black Mountains and the Great Craggies. From here each range builds up to more than 6,000 feet. The Craggies taper down into the Swannanoa Valley on the southeast. The Blacks descend northward to Burnsville, N.C.

A forest of red spruce and Fraser fir borders the parking area. Red spruce, or "he-balsam," is the taller tree. Large specimens attain a height of one hundred feet. The wood has an excellent resonant quality utilized in making piano sounding boards, violins and other stringed instruments. A few of its many other uses include general construction, pulp, boxcar siding, and canoe ribbing.

RED SPRUCE

The smaller Fraser fir, thirty to forty feet, is a picturesque conifer of the highest elevations. Although seldom large enough to produce lumber, it holds the soil of the steep headwaters terrain and thereby protects the watersheds from erosion damage.

FRASER FIR

Known also as the "she-balsam" because of the milky resin that blisters and runs from the bark, the fir is further distinguished from the larger spruce by the bluish-green undersides of its needles and by its plump, upright cones. The hanging cones of the spruce are more slender and somewhat shorter, one and a half to two inches.

From the parking area, a wide path heads into the forest along the grade of an old lumber railway, operated 1911-19. Beneath the straight trunks of the conifers, the ground is covered with a spongy duff of needles, an accumulation of centuries. The recent layers cover old logs and stumps like a blanket. This is how Graveyard Fields on the Pisgah Ridge may have appeared before the region was seared by a great fire in 1925.

Enough sunlight reaches through to sustain a robust colony of American shield fern and northern lady fern. A veneer of mosses patches the tree trunks and old logs.

This is the forest type referred to as "Canadian," as it is representative of the spruce-fir forests that cover vast wilderness areas of our good neighbor to the North. There the trees cover broad, moist lowlands. The same climate is repeated in these Carolina mountains where high altitude brings cool temperatures and abundant moisture.

Cotton Tree Gap
*361.1 miles
elev. 5,141*

Beard-like tufts of cotton-moss, a light green lichen, grow from the trees, "just a-hangin' and a-fannin'." They resemble the Spanish moss of the American subtropics but are not even distantly related. Spanish moss is a member of the pineapple family.

View of Glassmine Falls
361.2 miles
elev. 5,197

A "wet weather" falls cascades like a ribbon of white foam two hundred feet down the face of Horse Range Ridge. Near the base of the falls, the glint of a mica dump locates the old Abernathy mine and the cabin site of Will Arwood. During the early 1900s, Will pick-and-shoveled the "glass" into sacks and packed it over the mountains by mule to Micaville in the Toe River Valley.

Mica was once commonly known as isinglass, generally abbreviated in the mountains to "glass."

View of Graybeard Mountain
363.4 miles
elev. 5,592

yellow buckeye	hawthorne
beech	highbush
yellow birch	blueberry
mountain ash	

Graybeard (elev. 5,365) is a prominent peak on the Blue Ridge, seen directly across the Swannanoa headwaters of the Asheville watershed. Native lowlanders have long looked to Graybeard as a weather prophet. The appearance of rain is often heralded by a gray fleece of clouds bearding the mountain's summit.

BEECH

YELLOW BIRCH

YELLOW BUCKEYE

Depending on whether you are driving north or south, Graybeard is your first or last closeup of the Blue Ridge. The pinnacle is prominent on the crest line to the left of Graybeard, and in the far left the Black Mountains reveal the Parkway like a swathe through the dark spruce.

The overlook rests along the flats of a high mountain "bench" between "snurly, burly" Bullhead on the left, (elev. 5,925) and Craggy Dome (elev. 6,085) on the right. The bench is covered with a brushlike forest of squat trees over two hundred years old known as the Peach Orchard. The orchard consists almost entirely of beech, yellow birch, and yellow buckeye whipped and stunted by the wind. Few shrubs grow beneath the trees and the ground is covered with a rank, native grass.

The Peach Orchard is actually a mountain glade, a forest type typical of the rain-drenched benches and high slopes. It is remarkably similar to the Apple Orchard atop Apple Orchard Mountain in Virginia. The latter, however, is an almost solid stand of northern red oak.

View of Craggy Dome
364.1 miles
elev. 5,640

The Craggy Gardens of catawba rhododendron cover the foreground slopes and reach almost to the summit of Craggy Dome (elev. 6,085) on the right. Each mid-June the red-purple flowers open in splendid profusion over the broad backbone of the Great Craggies. It is one of the signal events of summer and attracts an ever increasing number of visitors.

The mass of rhododendron is channeled with narrow openings covered with tall grass. They have the appearance of pathways through the tidy rhododendron clumps and give reason for the name of gardens.

Craggy Gardens is a large heath bald covering several hundred acres on the high slopes of Craggy Dome, Craggy Pinnacle, and Craggy Knob. The name "bald" refers to the smooth appearance of the mountain as compared to that of a forested crown. Heaths are primarily a group of acid-soil shrubs found abundantly in the mountains, that frequently grow in dense associations on high or exposed locations.

CATAWBA RHODODENDRON

If you should hike through the gardens you would find the mountain laurel, blueberry, mountain cranberry, and minniebush. They, like the rhododendron, are members of the heath family of plants.

A small tree, the mountain ash, is found among the heaths, particularly around the overlook. In fall its twigs are loaded with glistening red berries. Other trees, following the lead of the mountain ash, are gradually encroaching on the Craggy Gardens. Eventually it may become another "Peach Orchard" of beech, birch, and buckeye.

One explanation for the heath balds is that the trees were originally burned off by the Indians to attract game. The land soon grew into a grass meadow or bald. In time the grass was crowded out by the heaths.

The view from the overlook reaches from the slopes of Craggy Pinnacle across several ridges to the western chain of the Black Mountains.

The **Craggy Pinnacle Tunnel** is 245 feet long. *364.4 miles.*

View from Pinnacle Gap
364.6 miles
elev. 5,497

Self-guiding nature trail; Craggy Visitor Center.

A long view of rumpled foothills vagabonds over the far-below. The far-below in this instance is the Ivy River Valley. Far beyond, the Bald Mountains tumble over themselves along the eastern edge of Tennessee.

The view is bordered by Craggy Flats on the left, and Craggy Pinnacle on the right. A self-guiding nature trail leads up to Craggy Flats rest shelter and beyond to Craggy Gardens picnic grounds.

A trail to the top of the Pinnacle (elev. 5,892) starts from the parking area at Craggy Dome, mile 364.1. Among the rocky crags atop the Pinnacle is the "camp rock" used by a hunter named Buckner during his trips through the region. The sharp profile of the Pinnacle, as seen from the Parkway, justifies its name. The folks in Buckner's day, however, saw the mountain from another point of view and called it Buckner's Butt.

The trails over these blustery mountains pass through natural gardens of catawba rhododendron and the fern-and-moss strewn forests of wind-twisted trees. On

the very top you can reach out and hold the world in your hands.

The Craggy Visitor Center contains exhibits describing the mountain "balds" and the natural heath gardens. The radiant beauty of rhododendron, mountain laurel, and azalea are presented in facsimile. Many "wild pretties" of the mountains are presssed and mounted in frames to aid you in their identification. Learning the names of wildflowers along the trails and roadside is a colorful way of acquiring a host of new friends.

The **Craggy Flats Tunnel** is 355 feet long. *365.5 miles.*

Bee Tree Gap
367.6 miles
elev. 4,900

HONEY BEE

Entrance to Craggy Gardens Picnic Grounds.

Bee Tree Gap lies at the head of Bee Tree Creek, a tributary of the Swannanoa River. During the late 1700s, when settlers first moved into the Swannanoa Valley below, a man discovered a bee tree along the creek. He felled the tree across the banks, and there it lay for many years after the bees were smoked out for their honey.

Bees, known to the Indians as "the white man's fly," were introduced to America during the colonization of the Atlantic seaboard. Escaping swarms spread westward into the forests and established themselves years before the pioneers.

Craggy Gardens
Recreation Area
700 acres
elev. 5,220

BEE BALM OR WILD BERGAMOT

Picnic grounds; rest rooms; drinking fountains; hiking trails.

The picnic grounds of Craggy Gardens are set in a grassy forest glade known as Bear Pen Gap. The bear pen is a combination deadfall and pen whereby the trapped bear could be confined until the trapper came by and shot it. The original bear pen has long since worn away.

Since the first settlement below the mountains, until as recently as the 1930s, cattle and sheep had free range on these grassy highlands. The steep land was beyond farming, but wild grass grew abundantly beneath squat, wind-brushed trees. A heavy annual rainfall of sixty inches or more keeps the highlands glades green, "no matter what the weather below."

The Pisgah National Forest borders Craggy Gardens on the north and western sides. Opposite is the Asheville Watershed, a forest preserve draining the slopes of the Great Craggies into blue-eyed reservoirs of crystal mountain water.

High altitude and plentiful rainfall give Craggy Gardens a wildflower variety all its own. In May and June the gardens warm up and join the highland display with blossoms that have opened six weeks earlier below the moun-

Craggy Dome

OSWEGO TEA

CONE FLOWER

tains: violet, toothwort, blackberry, may apple, giant chickweed, stonecrop, and hawthorn. Some, like the wild crabapple, pin cherry, mountain ash, and blue cohosh are more exclusively native to the highlands. The high altitude has a peculiar and gratifying effect on the blackberry. It blooms its attractive white in June, but the long stalks are smooth and barbless.

The bloom highlight, of course, comes in mid-June when the catawba rhododendron purples over the Craggy Mountain summits.

A trail from the picnic area leads northward into a portion of the Gardens. Along the way, robust clumps of American shield and northern lady fern arch beneath beech and birch trees dwarfed and rounded by the wind. Their rough bark is greened-over by lichens, mosses, and polypody fern. Some of the mosses look like diminutive trees, and one variety of pale green lichens (Cledonia) hangs from trunks and branches in a manner resembling Spanish moss.

During July, a time when most of the ground flowers along the Parkway are quiet and subdued, the entrance road and picnic wayside are at their loveliest. The tousled heads of red Oswego tea and lavender bergamot intermingle with yellow coneflowers, pink phlox, and orange turkscap lily.

Trees and Shrubs

yellow birch	*pin or*	*black cherry*
sweet or	*fire cherry*	*mountain ash*
black birch	*yellow buckeye*	*serviceberry*
beech	*sugar maple*	*wild crabapple*
	hawthorn	*highbush blueberry*

Birds

towhee	*robin*	*veery*
Carolina junco	*field sparrow*	*Canada warbler*

Potato Field Gap
368.2 miles
elev. 4,600

At Potato Field Gap, ''somebody growed taters there.'' Hollows and gaps in the high mountains frequently contain a moist, black loam, yielding a bumper crop of potatoes and other vegetables. Herders and farmers from the lowlands sometimes put in a garden and tended it at intervals through the summer.

View of Lane's Pinnacle
372.1 miles
elev. 3,890

The mountain wall lying length-long before you culminates in Lane's Pinnacle (elev..5,230) on the far left. Directly beyond and parallel to the foreground mountain wall lie the Great Craggies. Here, the range is not con-

CAROLINA JUNCO

spicuous for its size, but let your eyes follow the crest leftward to the small notch high and far away. The notch is the Parkway motor road amid the proudest summits of the Craggies.

On the far right, the long, undulant crest line of the Swannanoa Mountains forms the opposite border of the Swannanoa Valley.

Charles Lane, the first owner of the Pinnacle, mined ore from its north slope for his forge on nearby Reems Creek. Lane established his operation in response to a state act passed in 1788 giving three thousand acres, ''not fit for cultivation most convenient to the different [County] seats . . . to any person who will build and carry on . . . a set of iron works.'' This encouraged the development of many forges and furnaces in the Carolina mountains.

The iron workers at a typical forge smelted ore and limestone between glowing layers of charcoal. Cold air blasts from water-powered bellows kept the mass at molten heat. After a few hours the liquid iron settled to the bottom of the forge ''nest,'' while the impurities, or slag, floated on top.

The impurities were drawn off. Hammer-men, ''immense in their arms,'' operated a heavy hammer that pounded the iron further to rid it of foreign matter, and then returned it to the forge for reheating.

A final hammering shaped the iron into bars for use by local blacksmiths. In some instances the ends of the bars were turned up like the runners of a sled. Several of the bars were bound together and hauled by oxen to blacksmith-farmers. These versatile craftsmen had small shops where they hammered-and-tonged out wagon tires, ox and horse shoes, plow shares, harrow teeth, ax heads, and many other necessities for themselves and their neighbors.

View of Bull Creek Valley
373.8 miles
elev. 3,483

Bull Creek Valley directly below is a northern inlet of the Swannanoa Valley, a roaming, fertile lowland bounded on the far horizon by the Swannanoa Mountains.

In 1799, Joseph Rice, a recently arrived settler, sighted a bull buffalo walking along the creek. He took careful aim and squeezed the trigger. The powder charge boomed like a thunderclap and sent a lead ball thudding into the last buffalo recorded in North Carolina.

Buffalo were the first animals to be exterminated by the white hunter. At first they were so plentiful that a small hunting party with dogs could kill ten to twenty a day. The animals depended upon their noses rather than their weak eyes to warn them of danger, and men could approach within easy gun range providing they kept downwind. Once the buffalo whiffed the feared man-scent the entire herd broke into a gallop, away and out of sight.

BUFFALO

Bull Gap
375.3 miles
elev. 3,107

Bull Gap and Bull Mountain extending to the Lane's Pinnacle are both above Bull Creek and derive their names from the buffalo Joe Rice shot along the creek in 1799.

The bull probably came plodding along a centuries-old trail established by his ancestors across the mountains between the Swannanoa and French Broad River Valleys. A considerable network of buffalo trails, used by the Indian and later by the white pioneers, led between the piedmont and the salt licks and bluegrass meadows of Kentucky.

Some years after the first settlers had taken the best lands in the Swannanoa Valley, new-home seekers moved through Bull Gap into Beaverdam Valley, not far from the present city limits of Asheville. Enough of the wilderness still remained to make the trek a pioneer adventure. In the early 1800s the great grandfather of Parkway neighbor Ivan Hughey ''come across through Bull Gap. A panther followed him all the way over the mountain. He was comin' in a covered wagon and it was dark before he made it over. He struck at it time and again with his bull whip.''

View of Tanbark Ridge
376.7 miles
elev. 2,782

Tanbark Ridge ''thumbs'' into the left foreground from Swan Mountain just beyond. On the far left horizon, three peaks—High Swan, High Knob, and Lane's Pinnacle—point out the Parkway route northward to the Great Craggies. The name Swan Mountain is probably derived from the nearby Swannanoa River.

Tanbark Ridge, also known as Tanyard Ridge, was once the site of an old family tannery. ''Way it got its name, this ole slave had a tanning outfit up on that ridge. George—he never had no other name, tanned for my grandpa and he [Grandpa] made shoes for the whole family—and harness. He kept a lot of horses. They used wooden pegs to half sole the shoes whittled out of white oak. George is buried under a tree on Bull Creek.''

Ivan Hughey, the teller of the above tale, remembered much about the early days in Bull Creek Valley. ''When my grandfather moved in there the nearest store was Augusta, Georgia. The people would git up a wagon train maybe onest or twicest a year. Before they'd git ready to go they'd put a man on a horse and he'd go around and warn the others.

''But it took days 'cause these mountains was thinly settled. Then they'd git together some'ers and make up a wagon train. Each man would have to have a lead horse that wasn't afraid of water. They'd take apples and other things to sell and bring back salt, soda, sugar, and coffee. If they run out before the next trip, they'd just have to do without.

''They horse-swapped all the way. Grandpa started out with a couple of horses and come home with a whole string. In them days they's always swappin'. You could swap a good flint-lock rifle for a whole farm.'' (1954)

Craven Gap
377.4 miles
elev. 3,123
Junction with N.C.
697; 7 miles to
Asheville

When we asked Uncle Newt, "How come Craven Gap to get its name?" he looked right thoughty and his blue eyes took on the color of the far-off skies. He puffed his pipe fur a middlin' while and then discovered it wasn't lit.

"Well, now, I'll tell ye," he says, knockin' out the ashes agin his knee, "all ever I heard tell of was this Craven feller did a heap of travelin', haulin' his wagon through the gap. Can't say he ever lived there and never knowed him either. He was long afore my time."

The Folk Art
Center
382.0 miles
Southern Highlands
Handicraft Guild

The Folk Art Center is a spacious and impressive building of native stone and wood. The Center offers workshops, and contains exhibits and a wide variety of handicraft and art work in its sale area. An indoor-outdoor auditorium provides space for lectures, films, dance exhibitions, and music. A library is available for study and research.

The center also includes a sales outlet of the Eastern National Parks and Monuments Association with a large selection of books on the Southern Highlands. Just adjacent is the Blue Ridge Parkway information desk with Park Service staff to tell you about the Folk Art Center and places to visit on the Parkway.

Asheville District
Ranger Station
382.3 miles

Intersection with
U.S. 70 at Oteen,
N.C.
382.4 miles

Asheville, 5 miles west; Black Mountain, 10 miles east.
As stated in an article in the Oteen *Skylight,* (December 11, 1924): "The town of Oteen is named for the large army hospital centered in its midst. The hospital was built shortly after World War I. Colonel Hoagland, the first commanding officer, dubbed it 'Oteen' from an Indian word meaning 'chief aim.' The 'chief aim' of each patient, of course, should be to get well."

Asheville

Named in 1793 for Samuel Ashe, a prominent jurist, Asheville is a city with a skyline of temples on a meandering plateau that guides the course of the French Broad.

Some of the temples house commercial and civic offices; others play host to thousands of visitors who vacation in this capital city of the sky.

Above and beyond the city lies a roaming skyline of mountain ranges: the Swannanoas, Blacks, Craggies, Blue Ridge, Newfounds, and Balds. The summits and slopes are green with timber. The valleys between are green with pastures, row crops, and apple orchards.

South of the city are clusters of modern factories: textile, chemical, electronic, glass, food, printing, and woodworking.

The city's great asset, however, is its scenic setting and mountain-cool climate. Asheville is an urban nugget in the heart of the highlands.

Throughout the green seasons vacationers fill the city's hotels, motor courts, and guest houses. "The Land of the Sky" holds forth with art exhibits, plays, music festivals, and handicraft fairs.

The handicraft fair draws native talent throughout the Southern Highlands: solemn Cherokee, patiently absorbed in basket weaving, unaware of the peering passersby; wood carvers, whittling out roosters, horse-heads, and lean, rifle-toting mountain men; handicrafters by their booths, displaying hooked rugs, coverlets, corn-shuck dolls, colonial chairs, wooden inlays, as well as silvercraft.

Evening programs of folk dances and songs that came to the mountains long ago and linger still. . .

> I wish I was a little sparrow,
>   Or a little bird that flies so high,
> I'd fly away to my true lover,
>   And in his breast so close I'd lie.

Folk Art Center

Parkway Guide

Between Asheville and the Great Smokies the Parkway rides Pisgah Ledge, with long ranges banking the sides of forested valleys. Here, no mountain, not even Mt. Pisgah itself, stands out so resolute as the massive solitaire of Cold Mountain.

At Tennessee Bald the Parkway changes its southwesterly direction and cruises northwest over the crest of the Great Balsams. League-long spurs reach far on either side into the valleys of the Tuckaseigee and Pigeon Rivers.

The most far-reaching of these wing-like spurs is the Plott Balsam, pointing to the outward distance toward tier upon tier of mountain ranges roaming in parallel with the Parkway. Beyond the Tuckaseigee River are the Cowee Mountains, and beyond them, the Nantahalas. On the opposite side, the Parkway view looks into the Newfound Range and the Cataloochee Balsams.

The names are, perhaps, incidental to the view, yet they have a colorful, venerable quality befitting the scenic climax of this roadway through a mountain wonderland. The names are those of the Cherokee, the people who fought with courage and desperation against the equally courageous resolve of the white invader. The Indians lost, but the melody of their sibilant tongue crowns the high peaks.

Perhaps they didn't lose. Not entirely. At the entrance to Great Smoky Mountains National Park lies the Qualla Reservation of the Eastern Cherokee. Several thousand Cherokee farm and hunt on the land of their fathers.

Swannanoa River
383.5 miles
elev. 2,040

Southern Railway and Interstate 40 cross.

The Swannanoa heads in the Blue Ridge and flows westward between the Great Craggies and the Swannanoa Mountains into the French Broad, five miles downstream from this point.

In the early 1700s the Shawano, or Shawnee Indians, had a town near the mouth of the river. Sometime during the middle of the century they joined in the general exodus of their tribe from the South to the Ohio River region. Although the town was abandoned before the coming of permanent white settlers, the site was well known to hunters and traders as "Swannano."

This name soon applied to the river and to the mountain range forming the south border of the Swannanoa Valley.

The first permanent settler on the lower Swannanoa, Samuel Davidson, built a cabin on Christian Creek, a nearby tributary. He came from the outpost of Old Fort east of the mountains with his wife, infant child, and a black woman slave.

PITCH PINE

One morning not long after his arrival, he went to search for his horse. From the cabin his wife heard the boom of flintlocks and, fearing the worst, she fled with her child and the slave. The terrified trio hurried on foot to Old Fort, seventeen miles away, where Mrs. Davidson told her fears to the riflemen. A group set out and discovered Davidson, scalped and dead near his cabin on Jones Mountain. An aged gravestone now bears the tale: "Here Lies Samuel Davidson, First White Settler of Western North Carolina. Killed Here by Cherokee, 1784."

The Indians had captured his horse and removed a bell Davidson kept on its neck. By ringing the bell they lured him into ambush.

The riflemen took up the Cherokee trail and fought a running battle along the Swannanoa that made the death of Davidson a costly sortie for the Indians.

Intersection with
U.S. 25
388.1 miles
elev. 2,217

Asheville, 5.5 miles north; Hendersonville, 15 miles south.

Biltmore Estate

Between U.S. 25 and the French Broad River, the Parkway passes through a wooded portion of the twelve thousand-acre Biltmore Estate. The entrance road, 3.5 miles north of the Parkway on U.S. 25, leads to Biltmore House, the great country mansion of George W. Vanderbilt.

Completed in 1895 after five years of intensive construction, the mansion reflects "in many details the lines of French Renaissance chateaux, particularly those of Blois and Chambord.'' The spacious rooms contain period furniture and art objects from a wide representation of the world's cultural centers. The gardens, lavish with azaleas, are a showy sequence of blossoms, spring through fall. Admission fee.

N.C. Highway 191
393.6 miles

Asheville, 9 miles north; Hendersonville, 17 miles southeast on N.C. 191; Brevard, 26 miles southwest on N.C. 191 and N.C. 280. Interstate 26 entrance 2.5 miles north on N.C. 191, or 4 miles south via N.C. 191 and N.C. 280.

View of rench Broad River
393.8 miles
elev. 2,000

During the first half of the eighteenth century the southern colonies engaged in a profitable fur trade with the Cherokee. Pack horses and Indian bearers carried fur loads from the Indian villages among the Balsam and Great Smoky Mountains to the white settlements in the East.

Several of the trading paths crossed the upper valley of the French Broad, entering from or near the present South Carolina line. The river probably derived the name ''Broad'' from hunters and traders who viewed the wide lowlands spreading away from its banks. They called it the ''French'' Broad to distinguish it from another river known as the Broad flowing down the east side of the Blue Ridge through English territory to the Atlantic.

The French claimed all the land drained by westward flowing streams entering into the Gulf of Mexico. They relinquished those claims to the English in 1763 at the close of the French and Indian War.

The French Broad rolls north and westward through the heart of the southern Appalachians. Its banks gradually deepen into a precipitous gorge as the big river tumbles and foams through the Bald Mountain range and enters the Great Valley of Tennessee.

Assuming a more leisurely pace, it gathers the Pigeon and the Nolichucky, and the united waters feed the Great Douglas Dam of the Tennessee Valley Authority. Beyond this massive reservoir the French Broad flows into the Holston at Knoxville to form the Tennessee.

SYCAMORE

PIGNUT HICKORY

Pisgah District, Pisgah National Forest
393-455.7 miles
elev. 2,000-6,410

The French Broad marks a point of entry into the Pisgah District of Pisgah National Forest. From the sycamore, river birch, and willows by the river's edge, the Parkway heads up-mountain along Shut-in Ridge with a forest boundary of oak, hickory, and pine.

The nucleus of Pisgah District consists of eighty-seven thousand acres acquired from the George Vanderbilt estate and put under administration in 1916. The present district total approximates one hundred and fifty thousand acres.

Under the direction of Dr. Carl A. Schenck, in the years 1898-1913, the Vanderbilt, or "Biltmore" forests were managed according to the precepts of scientific forestry. The prevailing methods of that day involved tremendous waste and backbreaking effort.

Dr. Schenck believed in a motto that stated, "Forestry is business; the best business is that forestry which pays best—in the long run." The practices of selective cutting, replanting, and reinvesting a portion of the revenues into roads and other facilities proved themselves in the Pisgah wilds.

Another wise forest practice that reaps untold recreation dividends today began in Pisgah during this same period with the stocking of deer, trout, and turkey. A system of game protector lodges, modeled after those found in the Black Forest of Dr. Schenck's native Germany, guarded the wildlife. Regionally, this was a novel practice. Today, with the exception of a few hundred acres, the entire district is a wildlife management area.

Water, a resource of vastly increasing importance, is still another vital reserve protected by the National Forest Service. Approximately 100 million gallons of water are consumed daily by the population and industries of the adjacent areas.

Forest, wildlife, and water are protected as one. Fire is the enemy.

CHESTNUT OAK

SCARLET OAK

Hiking Trail
394 miles

Thirteen mile Shut-in Trail follows the ridge line parallel to the Parkway from French Broad River Overlook, mile 394, to Mt. Pisgah Parking Area, mile 407.

View Down Walnut Cove to French Broad Valley
396.4 miles
elev. 2,915

The black walnut is found occasionally among the mountain hardwoods, but it thrives in throngs within the moist, rich soil of coves and hollows. Walnut is recognized by its dark bark and compound leaves similar to those of the sumac. In autumn the leaves contribute little to the lavish color shown by the other hardwoods. But unique and conspicuous are the bushels of dangling walnuts that embellish the naked branches.

In the mountains black walnut was used for homemade furniture and gunstocks. The inner bark, root, and hulls make a dark brown dye. Present day mountain handicrafters perpetuate the old crafts and dye wool from the ooze of boiled walnut. The wool is dipped repeatedly until the proper color is attained.

The Hendersonville Watershed

The forested basin viewed from Walnut Cove and Chestnut Cove overlooks includes the thirteen thousand-acre Hendersonville watershed. The city has obtained its

French Broad River

Walnut Cove Valley Overlook

water from this portion of the Pisgah National Forest since 1923. A special use permit issued in 1926 enabled construction of two separate intake dams with pipelines extending seventeen miles to Hendersonville. This course provides an average 4 million gallons per day (MGD), which is supplemented by water from Mills River to provide an average water demand of 5.5 MGD. The city water system serves most of the populated areas of Henderson County, totaling thirty thousand persons.

The watershed, as of July 1980, has been opened to the public for limited recreational activities. Anticipated uses are hunting, fishing, and hiking, in accordance with North Carolina health regulations. Since all water withdrawn from Pisgah National Forest is treated at the city water plant, any risk of contamination of the water supply is virtually eliminated. *(Water and Sewer Dept., City of Hendersonville, N.C., 1980)*

The **Grassy Knob Tunnel** is 802 feet long. *397.2 miles.*

Sleepy Gap
397.3 miles
elev. 2,920
Picnic table

Evidently Sleepy Gap is a good place to camp out, for the old time woodsmen "had'm a place to camp out there." Perry Davis, the ruddy-faced local lorist of the "Pisgie" country, gives an instance. "You know how come 'Sleepy' to get its name? Well, now, I'll tell ye. They was a man in there a-huntin'. He laid down there and just dropped off to sleep. I don't know who the man was, but it was 'way back."

Chestnut Cove Overlook
398.3 miles
elev. 3,035
Picnic table

No tree ever responded more vigorously to Appalachian climate than the American chestnut. It ranged from Maine to Georgia. In the Southern Highlands it covered entire slopes.

The cove once bore a heavy growth of chestnut. A few sprouts still stubbornly resist the fungus blight of the 1930s that withered trees into barkless skeletons, forlorn as in the wake of a forest fire.

Will the chestnut ever win its fight to survive? The issue is in doubt but not hopeless. A skirmish is being waged just below the overlook. Chestnut sprouts, green with vigor, rise from the stumps of blighted trees. Many do not survive a year. The light brown of newly dead leaves marks the end of a chestnut hope. But some cling to life long enough to bloom and grow bristly burrs with ripe nuts.

The sprouts of Chestnut Cove are not giving up.

CHESTNUT

Pine Mountain Tunnel
399.3-399.5 miles
1 462 feet

The longest of 26 tunnels probing through the hard mountain rocks.

In the early 1960s, work crews operated air drills, boring a pattern of long holes that were packed with explosives. The resounding boom shattered the rock into a "muck" that was scooped up by bucket loaders and trucked away. The cleared portion of the tunnel was braced with supports and the process repeated until the tunnel ended in daylight.

All but one tunnel are located in North Carolina between Little Switzerland Tunnel, mile 333.4, and Sherrill Cove Tunnel, mile 366.2 near the entrance to Great Smoky Mountains National Park. The twenty-six tunnels comprise a total length of 11,894 feet, or 2.25 miles.

The rough-winged swallow has adopted many of the tunnels as a nesting site. Drab brown and graceful, they are the most solitary of the swallows. Seldom more than one nesting pair dives and sweeps for insect prey about a tunnel entrance.

View of Pisgah Ledge
399.7 miles
elev. 3,350

Pisgah Ledge forms the central horizon with broad-domed Mount Pisgah marking its high point. The Parkway motor road follows the long reach of Pisgah Ledge southwest 23.5 miles to its junction with the Great Balsam Range at Tanasee Bald.

Pisgah and the level ridge extending from its left form "Pisgah and the Rat," a favorite landmark to local residents.

Bent Creek Gap
400.3 miles
elev. 3,270

Bent Creek, a meandering tributary of the French Broad, flows down the north slope of Pisgah Ledge and passes through Bent Creek Experimental Forest, Pisgah National Forest. An important long-range study is in progress observing the effects of clear cutting or "evenage silviculture" on the regional forests. This method is economically sound, at least for the short term. The ensuing years will evaluate the long-term merits.

Triplet Tunnels through Ferrin Knob
400.9-401.5

The coves and hollows on the south, or Wash Creek, side of Ferrin Knob are "pretty heavy with ferrins" (ferns).

View down Wash Creek Valley
401 miles

Wash Creek heads below the overlook and scoots down alongside Trace Ridge on the right. A trace or trail follows the ridge crest from nearby Beaver Dam Gap to the lowlands.

Wash Creek, like many headwater streams draining steep Pisgah Ledge, swells into a freshet or "wash" during heavy rains. After the torrent ceases, it subsides to a purling brook, all "washed out."

Beaverdam Gap
401.7 miles
elev. 3,570

Beaverdam Creek flows north from the Gap en route to the French Broad by way of Hominy Creek. Beaver were very common during the time of the Indian. Pelts comprised an important item of trade. Gradually the animals were hunted and trapped to extinction. Beaver in the Pisgah were exterminated about 1910 and had disappeared in most areas long before that.

The **Young Pisgah Ridge Tunnel** is 418 feet long.
403 miles.

Fork Mountain Tunnel *392 feet*
403.9 miles

Almost every county in the Southern Appalachians has a Fork Mountain. All rise between two converging forks of a stream. This Fork Mountain is bordered by Glady Fork on the east and Ballard Creek on the west.

View of Hominy Valley
404.2 miles

"Hominy grits" is a breakfast staple that sets a man right for a day's work. Ground from whole kernel corn and served steaming hot, grits is a constant side dish. A man may have bacon and eggs, he may have pancakes, cereal, or sausage. He'll always have his grits.

View of Mills River Valley
404.5 miles
elev. 4,085

Mills River Valley reaches into the Pisgah Highlands from the wide flats of the French Broad River beyond. Mills River gathers nourishment from countless mountain tributaries, and though its journey is a short one, enters the French Broad as a fine, wide stream.

SOURWOOD

William Mills, 1746-1843, came from the East to hunt along its banks. Like his widely separated neighbors, he depended on his skill with the flintlock to keep the meat-house full. One day in the early 1800s he spotted an elk near the river. Like the buffalo shot in 1799 by Joe Rice, it was the last of its kind reported in North Carolina.

red oak	*sourwood*
black oak	*pignut*
black locust	*mountain laurel*
cucumber tree	

Cutthroat Gap
405.5 miles
elev. 4,235

Junction with N.C. 151; 19 miles northeast to Asheville.
Wintry winds whip into the gap with cutting severity. A cold, cold place in winter time. "How hit got its name was on account of the wind blowing so hard through there. Hit just reaches plumb through from the North Pole."
(George Washington Mullinox, Mills River, N.C., 1954)

The gap is also referred to as Elk Pasture Gap, recalling a time when a small herd acquired by Mr. Vanderbilt from Yellowstone National Park was located nearby.

The **Little Pisgah Ridge Tunnel** is 583 feet long.
406.9 miles.

The **Buck Spring Tunnel** is 468 feet long. *407.1 miles.*

View of Mount Pisgah
407.4 miles
elev. 5,721

"Old Pisgie" rises big and bold on the right. From Mount Pisgah, Moses of the Hebrews first viewed the river Jordan and the Promised Land after he had led his people out of captivity in Egypt. A gun-toting, Bible-quoting preacher, James Hall, may have been the reverently inspired person who named Mt. Pisgah for its biblical ancestor. Hall came as a fighting chaplain among the twenty-four hundred Indian fighters of General Rutherford's expedition in 1776.

The naming of the mountain dates from this expedition, and the "Parson from Princeton" seems to be the source.

Rutherford's men saw the mountain probing skyward on the horizon from the French Broad Valley. All about them spread a game-rich, fertile, promised land.

Leaving the French Broad, they swung west over the Balsams and fell upon the Cherokee villages with devastating fury. After vanquishing their foes, they left for the war-torn East, but many vowed to return once they had settled the current business with the Redcoats of George III.

Following the Revolution, a resolute number of Rutherford's men came back and settled in their land of promise, with "Pisgie" big and bold on the horizon.

WHITE-TAILED DEER

Buck Spring Gap
407.7 miles
elev. 4,980

When George Washington Vanderbilt (1862-1914) came to Asheville in 1884, he "looked over Mount Pisgah way," and decided then and there to own the mountain. During the following years he quietly bought up one hundred thirty thousand acres, including his beloved Pisgah.

Buck Spring Gap, high on the mountain, marks the site of a rustic lodge where Vanderbilt entertained his famous guests. Artists, ambassadors, scholars, scientists, senators, and authors came to hunt, fish, hike, and relax.

Many years before, deer and other wildlife came to drink at Buck Spring, but in the 1890s game had been hunted almost out of existence. Vanderbilt restocked his wilderness refuge with deer, turkey, and trout. Their descendants thrive today.

Plans for the lodge were begun in 1896. The architects wished to build it of huge chestnut logs. These, however, were not at hand, and other trees, mainly yellow poplar, were used.

Vanderbilt might be described as an enlightened amateur in a variety of sciences and enterprises. He employed and encouraged a talented group of pioneers in the fields of forestry, dairying, and animal husbandry. A student of architecture and landscape gardening, he employed and worked with such men as Frederick Law Olmstead in completing his great country house at Biltmore.

WILD TURKEY

TROUT

Mount Pisgah from Overlook

Mount Pisgah Inn

Mount Pisgah Picnic Area
407.8 miles
elev. 4,900

Picnic tables (50); Comfort station.

Sept. 8, 1980.
408.0 miles

Timber Rattlesnake by the Roadside

The heavy body glides forward in slow, tight curves pushing the raised head peering hypnotically just above the grass. Sensor tongue flicks into the air for taste of prey or danger. A movement is caught by the searching eyes. Taut, with rattle raised and ready to strike, the snake pauses. The dark stare turns slowly to and fro. Nothing there. The head dips down and guides the body, quietly vanishing into the thicket. No one follows. But we remember the times we walked through grass and thicket too dense for our eyes to see our feet.

Flat Laurel Gap
408.4 miles
elev. 4,980

The upper limits of many mountain areas in the southern Appalachians are surprisingly level rather than uneven and rugged as we might suppose. The local "flats" have a dense evergreen cover of rhododendron or laurel.

CATAWBA RHODODENDRON

The flourish of rhododendron and other shrubs lays an evergreen thicket over a ground cover of crisp, dead leaves. Sounds are the drip by drip melody of fingerling streams, the scraping of leaves, the call of a secretive bird. This is the home of the salamander, the winter wren, and the red squirrel. Here is a place to enjoy your binoculars, hand lens, and nature books.

Mount Pisgah Inn
408.6 miles
elev. 4,925

52 rooms; restaurant; gift shop.

Mount Pisgah Inn is more than a place to stop; it is a destination. The miles of wilderness are suddenly enhanced by a haven for repose. Here is a place to call it a day. Relax with a full and leisurely meal. Indulge in the pleasures of good fellowship. Sleep is quiet as a moth's wing. Refreshing as sunrise.

Mount Pisgah Campground
408.8 miles
elev. 4,850

70 tent sites; 70 trailer sites; 100-seat theatre; rest rooms (no showers).

Forest Trees and Shrubs

northern red oak	*sweet or black birch*	*serviceberry*
chestnut oak	*yellow birch*	*eastern hemlock*
		red spruce

List continues

EASTERN OR CANADIAN HEMLOCK

Table Mountain pine
black locust
red maple
striped maple
mountain maple
chestnut sprouts
mountain ash
yellow buckeye
pin cherry
black cherry
beech
flame azalea
highbush blueberry
mountain cranberry
mountain laurel
rosebay rhododendron
catawba rhododendron
Carolina rhododendron
huckelberry
red-twig leucothoe
shonny haw or withe-rod viburnum
hobblebush viburnum
mountain winterberry
hawthorn
gooseberry
witch hazel
bush honeysuckle
wild hydrangea
purple-flowering raspberry
minnie bush
cinnamonbush

Ground flowers

Spring
golden groundsel
hawkweed
columbine
spiderwort
bluet
giant chickweed
violet

Summer

HOBBLEBUSH VIBURNUM

BLACK SNAKEROOT

galax
goatsbeard
meadow rue
fire pink
heal-all
southern mountain mint
wild bergamot
oswego tea
bluet
evening primrose
sundrop
fourleaf loosestrife
beard tongue
coreopsis
cutleaf coneflower
joe-pye weed
oxeye daisy
black-eyed susan
yarrow
daisy fleabane
phlox
black snakeroot or cohosh
pink turtlehead
blue-eyed grass
Turk's-cap lily
pokeberry

Fall
big leaf aster
accuminate aster
white wood aster
flat topped aster
goldenrod
gentian
thistle
sunflower
ox-eye

Common Ferns
cinnamon fern
interrupted fern
New York fern
American shield fern
lady fern
hay-scented fern

Birds and Mammals

LADY FERN

towhee
junco
rose-breasted grosbeak
chicadee
winter wren
white-breasted nuthatch
golden-crowned kinglet
veery
raven
red-tailed hawk
cooper's hawk
ruffed grouse
black bear
white-tailed deer
bobcat
red-squirrel

Frying Pan Gap
409.6 miles
elev. 4,931

Prior to 1893 when George Vanderbilt commenced buying an immense portion of the Pisgah wilderness and converting it into a game preserve, the folks of that time, or "old people," as they are referred to by the mountaineers, herded their livestock on the open forest range.

The herders had a camp at the Gap, still referred to on maps of the locality as "the camp grounds." The herders liked to camp right on the crest line within the shelter of the Gap. The high altitude gave good visibility and hearing, and cool comfort from the heat and insects of the lowlands. These favored campsites also had fine springs with clear, cold water.

The spring at this Gap had an odd shape, very like a frying pan. This may be the reason for its culinary name. But it is also known that the herders kept a frying pan as common property at the camp site. When not in use, the pan hung from a nearby tree for the next group of campers who "might happen by and put up for the night."

The **Frying Pan Tunnel** is 582 feet long. *410.1 miles.*

View from above the Pink Beds
410.3 miles
elev. 4,825

The Pink Beds contain an extensive understory forest of mountain laurel and rosebay rhododendron growing luxuriantly beneath a canopy of oak and other hardwoods. It extends over five miles of bottomlands, fifteen hundred feet below, between the Parkway and the ridge border beyond. During May and June the dark evergreenery of these shrubs backgrounds a display of glistening blossoms and captured sunlight.

The name Pink Beds probably derives from several sources. Pink is a common natural color. Beds of wild phlox formerly grew abundantly in the area. This field plant is an opportunist that may suddenly appear in great annual crowds, and then vanish like a gypsy. The pink of phlox is no longer common in the beds.

MOUNTAIN LAUREL

Another name source derives from a pink stone formerly quarried in the area. The pink of mountain laurel still remains, abundantly beautiful every spring.

Cradle of American Forestry
411 miles
elev. 4,710
viewed from Rich Mountain Overlook

At intervals, portions of U.S. 276 indicate its gradual descent down Pisgah Ledge leading to the scene of the woodland epic called Cradle of American Forestry. The story is told in the Pink Beds. It begins at the visitor center where movies and audio exhibits relate the saga of men like Dr. Carl Alwin Schenck who strove to make forestry the science and profession it is today. A reconstruction of the "First School of American Forestry" is near the visitor center. The replica is faithful to every detail provided from old photos and the memories of the students.

Cradle of Forestry Overlook

The U.S. Forest Service is working on a master plan to relate the story at several locations. Visitors will travel the Pink Beds by jeep caravan to exhibits of forestry, past and present. They will see the trout pools and fawn pens that grew from the energy of President Franklin D. Roosevelt's youthful Civilian Conservation Corps. They will see a span of logging history with an old logging camp and its steam locomotive, compared to modern harvesting and hauling by truck. They will see the Forest Service apply its concept of multiple land use for timber, outdoor recreation, and conservation of water and wildlife.

The tour, when fully complete, will take a day and cover a century.

For the present, it is memorable to visit the school and hear a near century-old portrayal of a lecture by Dr. Schenck. He is a tall, lean man, who lectures with restless, gesticulating energy. The ''high collar'' fashion of the Teuton professor contrasts with the open shirt informality of his students. But they are as one towards their mission in forestry.

George Vanderbilt, a confirmed conservationist, hired Dr. Schenck on the recommendation of the Chief Forester of England to manage the forests of his estate. Schenck accepted the position in his native Germany and came to America. The school was obviously the project nearest his heart.

From 1898 until 1913 the doctor trained 300 foresters. He and his Biltmore Forest School students were true pioneers. The men lived in cabins in the Pink Beds and had provisions hauled to them by wagon. On cool nights they were sometimes disturbed by the slithering of snakes through the warm, open rocks of the fireplace.

No adequate textbooks were available, so Dr. Schenck wrote an entire curriculum. Although he spoke and wrote English poorly at first, he soon overcame the handicap. When in doubt during lectures about a certain English word, he conveyed the idea by resorting to similar meanings contained in any of several languages he spoke fluently.

Classes were held in the forenoon. In the afternoon the entire group, including guest professors, saddled up and took to the field. Schenck rode Punch, a small, wiry horse barely high enough to keep the doctor's feet from touching the ground. When idle, this imposing steed stood with drooping head as though asleep. But the moment the doctor mounted and took the reins, Punch was off at a tireless trot.

Each year the students made several camping trips to study timbering methods. The wasteful practices of the day were an object lesson. Schenck taught that it was most profitable to log selectively as opposed to clear-cutting, and to put back a large part of the revenue into forest

TULIP TREE OR YELLOW POPLAR

WHITE ASH

improvement. Progress, however, improves on the pioneer. Modern forestry practice has departed from the series of selective cuttings taught by Dr. Schenck. Today a forest is harvested by one or more intermediate cuts followed by a final "regeneration cut" wherein an entire area is cleared.

Dr. Schenck, on memorable occasions, topped off the highly organized and practical course by taking his students on a tour of Germany to study methods in his homeland.

He taught that German forestry was suited to Germany and that American forests required methods suited to their locality. Methods successful in the hardwood-pine forests of the Southern Highlands might fail if applied to the hardwood-pine forests of Missouri.

After the closing of the forestry school in 1913, he returned to Germany. In 1951 the doctor visited Pisgah Forest and appreciatively read the bronze plaque erected in his honor by the alumni of the Biltmore Forest School on the site of the field headquarters in the Pink Beds.

His last years were ones of unsurpassed memories, reliving the birth of practical conservation that he and others like Gifford Pinchot helped to form and create. And memories of "his boys," who sang,

Who is the man on a horse named Punch,
Riding along at the head of the bunch
Giving no time to eat our lunch?

View of Cold Mountain
411.8 miles

A bold six thousand-foot cone among broad-shouldered mountain neighbors: "Hit's a mean place in winter. Hit's cold up thar."

A hunter, about a century ago, lost his footing and slid a fast, icy distance down the mountain. He returned unhurt to his companions and made known that the trip had been a cold one. This anecdote, according to historian F. A. Sondley, gave the mountain its descriptive name.

And "hit's still cold up thar." In the winter of 1962 the temperature reached lows of more than 20° below zero.

Wagon Road Gap
411.9 miles
elev. 4,535

Intersection with U.S. 276; north 22 miles to Waynesville; south 17 miles to Brevard.

The wagon road, like most mountain crossings within the Parkway region, began as a foot trail between opposing lowlands. Later, herders on the southeastern, or Brevard, side improved the trail sufficiently for two-wheeled wagons to haul salt and other provisions to the top. Eventually, the way was made suitable for large, four-wheeled wagons, hauling between Waynesville and Brevard.

Wagon Road Gap Parking Overlook
412.2 miles
elev. 4,550

Red oak, black oak, black or sweet birch, serviceberry.

August is a fortunate time to tarry here. The tousled head of bergamot mints dapple the grass with pink, purple, and white. Insects wing in to visit the scented flowers

Looking Glass Rock from Overlook

WILD BERGAMOT OR BEE BALM

and often find an eight-legged foe waiting in ambush. A species of crab spider lurks among the blossoms and preys upon the fragile flies that come for nectar. The crab spider spins no web but uses a single thread to anchor a leap to safety when something bigger than a fragile fly appears.

August is also bloom time for the southern mountain mint and the oxeye. The nearby miles are bordered by lavender-flecked mints with frost-white leaves. Oxeye are tall clumps of sunshine on a stem.

Pigeon Gap
412.5 miles
elev. 4,520

PASSENGER PIGEON

Flocks of the now-extinct passenger pigeons, so dense they darkened the sky, flew over the gap, crossing and recrossing to favorite feeding grounds where they fattened themselves on acorns, beechnuts, chestnuts, and various wild fruits.

The birds nested in extensive colonies, building their flimsy twig nests in the forest trees. Each parent raised a single fledgling that lived in daily peril of tumbling from its nest. The pigeons shifted their feeding and nesting grounds periodically to thwart the large numbers of predators that came to the easy banquet they provided. For many years after white hunters had killed off most of the big game, pigeons were a main source of meat for the Cherokee.

The last passenger pigeons were seen in this country around the turn of the century. Evidently they could survive only in huge flocks numbering hundreds of thousands and even millions. Once their numbers were reduced by market hunters and possibly parasites from domestic fowl, the great flocks melted into extinction.

**View from the Head
of
Pounding Mill
Branch**
413.2 miles
elev. 4,700

Pin cherry, northern red oak, red maple, black locust.
Front right and directly below, the young valley of Pounding Mill Branch slants sharply into the forested lowlands. In the straightaway the long, low outline of Rich Mountain stretches toward Frying Pan Mountain on the left and the bold surge of Looking Glass Mountain on the right.

Straight beyond, a second tier of mountains dips into the field-green patterns of the French Broad River Valley, outlined in the way-beyond by the misted, traveling outline of the Blue Ridge.

Would you like to imagine yourself into a century ago, walking downstream through the woods along Pounding Mill Branch? Below, yonder, where it's not so steep. It is a bright day, with sun-flecks dancing on the shadowed leaves. You listen to the bland enchantment of the ''tonkling'' stream and the wood thrush. They are pleasant, harmonious sounds.

Suddenly, your ears catch an odd ''k'splash, k'splash, k'thud!'' Perplexed, you pause, then move inquisitively nearer. ''K'splash, k'splash,'' the sound directs your eyes to a long wooden beam pounding down, "k'thud!," into a sturdy wooden box.

It's a pounding-mill, an old-timey contraption of the mountaineer for grinding his corn the lazy way. Water power operates a seesaw beam that pounds the corn.

One end of the beam has a water bucket. The stream pours into the upraised bucket, "k'splash," causing it to tilt down and dump the water, "k'splash." The now heavier hammer end of the beam whams down into the corn box, "k'thud!"

K'splash, k'splash, k'thud! K'splash, k'splash, k'thud!

It will take a whole day to grind enough corn to make a batch of corn bread. And maybe a chipmunk will climb in the bucket and become mincemeated. But all this is happening a hundred years ago and time and chipmunks "don't make no matter mind."

CHIPMUNK

Tunnel Gap
415.6 miles
elev. 4,325

During the early 1900s a pioneering railroader proposed a line between Waynesville, N.C. and Greenville, S.C. He planned to move upstream along a fork of the Pigeon River and tunnel beneath the mountains at what has come to be known as Tunnel Gap. The railroad came to naught, but portions of the grade were formerly utilized by logging trains and now by U.S. 276 and the Forest Service.

The Monarch Butterfly

MONARCH BUTTERFLY

Through September, the orange-brown, black-striped monarch butterflies migrate southwest along the Blue Ridge. They cross Pisgah Ledge north to south at several points but show an apparent preference for Tunnel Gap. Here the ledge is narrow and affords a short crossing between the massive hollows on either side.

These are the eastern monarchs and come from all points in southern Canada and the states east of the Rockies. Their destination is a narrow region in the high plateaus of central Mexico. Here they overwinter by the millions on branches and trunks of tall mountain evergreens. Beneath the trees, they carpet the forest floor.

Monarchs produce several generations in their summer habitat. The final generation includes females with dormant ovaries. The energies of these and the accompanying males are conserved for the arduous migration.

Who would believe the wings of a butterfly could best the rigors of a journey from Canada to Mexico? Many of them don't. Storms and other hazards deplete their ranks; bird migrants harass and devour them. The monarch migration coincides with that of the broad-winged hawks. High above they can be seen making pass after pass into a fluttering array of monarchs.

They reach Mexico in November and reside in semi-dormancy until late January, responding to a temperature range from just below to moderately above freezing. As the days begin to lengthen, the monarchs open their wings to increasing warmth and begin to stir. Soon they spring into flight and mingle cloudlike above the trees. With evening they return to roost.

This preamble is shortly followed by an outpouring northward. By early February most are headed toward the patches of milkweed that nourished them as caterpillars.

Many of the females have mated. On the way they pause to deposit eggs on local milkweed. Progeny from this generation may continue northward, or may remain where they were born.

For some the destination may be Texas; others press gradually onward until they reach into Canada in June. Some of the end point monarchs are resplendently new. These are probably of the most recent generation born en route. Others are tattered and travel torn. Did this ragged remnant complete the entire journey to Mexico and return? *(This information was obtained from Dr. and Mrs. F.A. Urquart, college professors, whose decades of travel, coordinating, and research led to the discovery of "The Monarch's Mexican Haven," published in* National Geographic, *Vol. 150, No. 2, August 1976.)*

View into Cherry Cove
415.7 miles
Roadside easel: The Migrating Monarch

BLACK CHERRY

The Cove lies 1,000 feet below the overlook. In such cool, moist sites the black cherry grows to giant size. In its typical habitat of old fields or as an occasional "loner" in the forest, the tree averages a mere fifty to sixty feet in height. In favorable sites like Cherry Cove it reaches a hundred feet or more. The trunks, three and even four feet through, rise like a group of black columns.

The black cherry of the country roadside and old fields is humble in comparison and hardly seems the same tree. More than any other plant it becomes the browsing grounds of the tent caterpillar. Frequently these voracious feeders strip every leaf to the ribs and force the tree to produce a new crop. The cove trees, however, are seldom chewed by these creeping campers.

In May and June the trees blossom with spindle-shaped clusters of small white flowers. By July and August they mature into red-black fruits, often so much a bumper crop that they hide the leaves. The juicy fruits are eagerly eaten by birds. Over seventy species are known to feed upon them. Birds are an important means of distributing the seed. They digest the soft part of the fruit and pass the hard, indigestible pits.

The finished wood of black cherry becomes darker and richer with age and rivals walnut for paneling and furniture. High mountain coves are among the few places with trees of size for lumber.

Both the black cherry and the locally abundant pin cherry grow at John Rock overlook, mile 419.4.

View into Log Hollow
416.3 miles
elev. 4,445

northern red oak	*cucumber magnolia*	*silver bell*
chestnut oak	*mountain laurel*	*red maple*
fraser magnolia		

During the 1880s the long-drawn cry of "Timber!" resounded on the slopes of Pisgah Ledge, as a tall, straight forest giant toppled in a graceful arc and slammed to earth. With a final, jarring bounce and roll, the felled tree came to rest. As the dust settled and silence returned, lumbermen axed away the limbs and sawed the trunk.

Shouting the warning "Ball-hoot!" men dug their cant-hooks into the logs and sent them sliding and crashing into a "jackpot" of logs in the hollow below.

Lumberjacks worked the logs into a stream bed with their versatile cant-hooks, building up a freight of logs to be sluiced downstream. At an appointed hour, men on several feeder streams released the "splash-dam" gates and sent a flood of converging waters down the mountain carrying the logs to the mill.

Bridges Camp Gap
416.8 miles
elev. 4,450

A man named Bridges once lived in the Pink Beds. He owned land at the gap where he maintained a cabin as his "headquarters" while away from home hunting or tending his livestock.

Fraser Magnolia

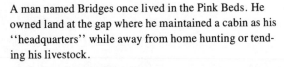

In May the languid, white blossoms of the Fraser magnolia bring a touch of the tropics to a forest whose leaves are just emerging, seemingly as out of place and unexpected as they are lovely to behold. The magnolia group are very ancient plants that spread northward from tropical regions. Named for John Fraser (1750-1811), a Scottish botanist who found these mountains a happy hunting ground, the Fraser magnolia thrives in response to the heavy annual rainfall. In August the cone-shaped fruit shows as tints of pink among the leaves. The fruit contains bright red seeds that squeeze out and drop to the ground.

FRASER MAGNOLIA

View of Looking Glass Rock
417.1 miles
elev. 4,493
John Rock and Cedar Rock Mountain on right

silver bell	*red maple*
red spruce	*black locust*
northern red oak	*witch hazel*

In winter, water caught by a freeze congeals like a glassy veneer to the cliff and reflects a dazzle of sunlight. Spring and wet weather also "mirror" the sunbeams.

The Looking Glass, a broad four-hundred-foot cliff massive in comparison to the lowlands around it, faces the Parkway. Its 3,969-foot elevation, however, is more than five hundred feet lower than the overlook.

The hard granite of the Looking Glass stands in a basin carved by scouring mountain streams. The surrounding foothills are composed of gneiss, a comparatively softer rock. The persistent, unhurried methods of erosion gradually wear away the gneiss more rapidly than the granite and carve the Looking Glass in bold relief.

Like the Pink Beds and Mount Pisgah, the Looking Glass Rock is well known and well storied by local residents. As told by Samuel Hale Seniard, "A lots of 'em goes up there to see it. My granddaddy and a bunch of these mountain men measured it with a chain. Hit come out seven miles around. Thur's a trail up the back to the Cold Spring right on top.

WITCH HAZEL

"A way back they cut the timber and let it off by cable. Vanderbilt never went in much for cuttin' timber, but he built a ladder up the Looking Glass. His men bored holes and then drove these locust pins in the rock and fastened thur rounds (rungs) to them. They used it for eight or ten years and then they took it apart to keep somebody from hurting themselves."

Seniard Gap
417.8 miles
elev. 4,775

Sam Seniard drove a cab in Brevard, N.C., below the mountains. One summer day in 1954 we visited Sam at his cab stand and he obliged with boyhood recollections about life along the Seniard Trail and at Seniard Gap.

"Hit was named for my grandfather, Gaston Seniard. He's been dead about twenty-five years. Died at ninety-six. He was in the Civil War. I don't know what he done in there but I believe he tole us he was a messenger and rode a horse.

"We been here close to a hundred years. He come in here when he was a young man. We used to drive a lot of cattle up here at the Gap. Let'm herd up there in summer and bring'm back down in autumn. We drove them along the Seniard Trail. Hit led from John Rock and Looking Glass Rock right up to the mountains. We had to ford the river fourteen times to get to the farm. Stayed up there four or five days or even a week. We growed potatoes, and corn, and beans. We went in a covered wagon and stopped along and fished at the fords. We has us a wooden tub fer to put the fish in. Up at the farm we penned part of the creek and put'm in for when we wanted a mess. We always brought home a tubful of fish to grandma."

TROUT

East Fork Overlook
418.3 miles
elev. 4,930

Yellowstone Falls, an infant cascade on the Pigeon River headwaters, spills down the edge of Rocky Bluff into a chasm shaggily covered with spruce and hemlock. The water-soaked rocks are draped with a yellowish moss and lichens that give reason for the name of Yellowstone.

Some mountain men who have tromped the country since boyhood would reply, "That haint it a-tall. Hit's knowed as yallerstone cause the rocks thar's got a yaller color to 'em."

Behind the overlook are impressive rock cuts, baring the stony innards of Pisgah Ledge. White stringers of quartz and feldspar run in cross hatches and bands through a darker group of minerals composed primarily of biotite mica.

View of Graveyard Fields and Graveyard Ridge
418.8 miles
elev. 5,115

catawba	*serviceberry*	*mountain*
rhododendron	*mountain ash*	*winterberry*
mountain laurel	*bush honeysuckle*	*ground pine*
red maple	*highbush*	*ground cedar*
pin cherry	*blueberry*	*yellow birch*

CATAWBA RHODODENDRON

MOUNTAIN LAUREL

Graveyard Ridge rises to 5,600 feet immediately in front, beyond the bog-like flats of Yellowstone Prong. Years ago, beyond the memory of anyone living, a tremendous "wind-blow" knocked down much of the spruce forest covering the ridge. The fallen trunks and the jagged stumps became covered and rounded over by the fallen needles of the spruce regrowth. For many years the odd mounds gave the appearance of a graveyard.

In 1925, the "Big Fire" cremated the living forest and the graveyard alike.

The trees and shrubs making the forest recovery on this mile-high level give it the appearance of the blueberry bogs of the northern Great Lakes region. Clumps of blueberry, bush honeysuckle, catawba rhododendron, mountain winterberry, mountain laurel, and serviceberry spread among open areas of coarse grass, trailed here and there with ground pine and ground cedar. Occasionally a red maple or yellow birch represents the returning forest.

The graveyard is now an outdoor snack bar for catbird, Carolina junco, flicker, the white-tailed deer and the black bear. And maybe ole buzz-tail the rattler.

The Big Fire

Along the Parkway between Tunnel Gap and Mt. Hardy, miles 416 to 424, the dark green spruce cover is sharply defined atop the mountains. There is no gradual intermingling of evergreens into hardwoods. The sharp contrast outlines a great fire that destoyed over 25,000 acres of high grade timber on Thanksgiving Eve, 1925.

Bill Bradley of Waynesville was logging superintendent of Suncrest Lumber Company, a large outfit that logged the Pisgah and Balsam Mountain forests on the upper Pigeon, 1913-1926. Within the now burned area they had four camps and about five hundred men.

Bill was in the fire from spark to ashes. "It was awfully dry that year. We had four or five locomotives running up there. Each one had a spark-arrester stack. We had two men following each train a-watchin' on a motor car to see there was no fire started. There was thousands of acres cut over with all this slash on it and lots of brush....

"We used every precaution but for some unknown rea-

MOUNTAIN HOLLY OR WINTERBERRY

son a little fire started, maybe a cigarette, over near Yellowstone Falls. The men got right on this fire and corralled it. They burned around it and got it out.

"We came back up to the top of the mountain where we had Camp 24 on Shining Rock Divide and Camp 20 between Big Sam and Little Sam Knob. The trains were headquartered at 20 and I planned to spend the night at 24 because I could see all over. Before I could get set for the night the camp foreman came and got me. A fire started way down the mountain on the Little East Fork side. The wind got to blowing and brought it up.

SERVICEBERRY

"The foreman went down one side of the camp and I the other, waking the men. By the time we got up to his shack the fire was all around us. The wind carried it from mountain to mountain. I called Camp 22, at the head of Yellowstone Falls. They couldn't fight it and had to get out of there.

"There was green timber between Shining Rock and where we were at 24 on Shining Rock Divide. Most of the men took off from there down Grassy Ridge trail to Little East Fork. I spent the night with one boy out there in the green timber. We could see what the fire was doin'.

"Next morning he and I went out to 23 at Shining Rock. All of a hundred men were gone but a few. There was no timber at the camp, so it wasn't in any danger. After breakfast I said, 'Bob, le's see if we kin get back through that and see what it's done.' It was too hot. Burned us out. We went half way to 24 and had to return.

"We took off for camp 20 on Sams Branch and made it. The men saved the camp by putting wet blankets over the buildings. They kept pouring water to it out of the branch. But all the food burned. A big Thanksgiving feed had been prepared. I remember joking with the cook that we better eat them turkeys before something happens to them. They were all burned.

"About ten o'clock a motor car came through from 20 and we go on it. Some of the trestles we crossed were about burned out and it was like riding a big dip in a rolly-coaster.

"At 24 the cook was the only one left. He spent the night in a 10,000 gallon water tank. He stood in it with his head just above the water. Almost caught pneumonia.

"Camps 22 and 24 burned out. We lost twelve trestles, and three million feet of logs that had been skidded up to the track ready to load, and five million feet of logs that were felled and ready to skid. All of Sam Knob burned. We'd been logging it for four years. It had a thick stand of spruce and not a rock showing. When the fire quit it had burned all the soil off.

"The fire burned from the head of Little East Fork on back to Sam's and over to Black Mountain. Biggest part was over in eight or ten hours, but it smoldered and the ground burned until it rained, maybe a couple of weeks later. Wood ashes washed into the streams and killed the fish. You could see them floating, belly up.

"We never did know how the fire started for sure, but it's believed to have been started by coon hunters, accidentally."

Trees replanted by the Forest Service have grown back very slowly, for the soil after the fire is pitifully thin. Raging heat burned off the humus except on a few high strips. Soil remaining after the burn washed away and exposed vast rocky slopes.

Nature's way of building back the humus has begun with blackberry briars and pin cherry, which add a thin layer of leaves each season. But a hundred years may be needed to restore the spongy soil required by these spruce-fir forests so rare in the Southern Highlands— destroyed in a few hours by a man's carelessness with fire or perhaps a cigarette.

View of John Rock 419.4 miles elev. 5,330		
red spruce	*fire or pin cherry*	*mountain laurel*
red oak		*witch hazel*
yellow birch	*mountain ash*	*hawthorn*
serviceberry	*withe-rod viburnum or shonny haw*	*highbush blueberry*
red maple		
black or sour gum		*lyonia*
	black cherry	*phlox*
black locust	*catawba rhododendron*	

"Perry, do you know how John Rock got its name?"

"How come John Rock to get hits name? Well now I'll jest tell ye. A white horse fell off it one time name of John."

"What?"

"That's what I said. That's all I ever heard." *(Perry Davis, Pisgah Forest, N.C., 1954)*

A "burst-open" view of John Rock is reached via a trial that leads from

A shrubby matting of low lyonia,

The resinous tang of red spruce,

The paired trunks of black cherry with their scaly bark,

The lisp of the cedar waxwing, the trill of the Carolina junco.

John Rock is a formation similar to the Looking Glass on the left and Cedar Rock Mountain on the right, with bare rock cliffs facing the Parkway. Although the least of the three in elevation, it is easy to see why the fall from the rock meant eternity for poor John.

Away to the right of the view is a long ridge building up to a prominent peak, then dropping abruptly to the lowlands. The high point is Pilot Knob, the *tsu-wa-telda* of the Cherokee, a name signifying "that which points out."

Two native trees grow at this overlook: the pin

cherry stands in the island between the parking area and the motor road; the black cherry is at the beginning of the trail leading to the view of John Rock, next to the spruce. Compare the bark and leaves of the two cherries.

Balsam Spring Gap
420.2 miles
elev. 5,550

The spring source is a shallow depression high up in the spruce country. Balsam is the regional name for both the native Fraser fir and for the red spruce. To the mountaineer the former is the she-balsam; the latter the he-balsam.

Spur road to
Shining Rock
Wilderness
420.2 miles

This 18,500 acre wilderness in the Pisgah National Forest is part of the National Wilderness Preservation System. The wilderness is available by foot trails to hiker and nature lover. Within the pristine wilds, commercial timber cuttings, roads, motor travel, and permanent developments are not permitted.

Old Silver Mine
421 miles

Close by the motor road on the right side as you drive toward the Smokies was a shaft fifty to sixty feet deep on the slope of Silvermine Bald. It was worked at times from the late 1800s into the early 1900s. The mine didn't produce enough silver to make anyone rich, but the pay dirt kept the men digging and hoping.

The Southern Appalachians are peculiarly noted for ores in "specimen," rather than abundant quantities. A survey will reveal abandoned silver, gold, copper, arsenic, tin, and manganese mines, to name a few.

Fetterbush
Overlook
421.7 miles

Fraser fir, red spruce, fetterbush, bush honeysuckle.

The thick, matted branches of the fetterbush, or mountain pieris, have a way of fettering anyone who attempts to push through them. Even the mountain boomer, or red squirrel, "buzz-saws" in shrill protest when confronted with the cross-hatching of leaves and twigs. But the ruffed grouse feels secure within its shelter and pecks inquiringly for food among the fallen leaves. The fetterbush is an eager spring burst of white. Groups of small, urn-shaped flowers mingle among dark evergreen leaves.

The rich soil of Pisgah Ledge grows a thriving association of shrubs. Most belong to the heath family, which includes the abundant rhododendron, mountain laurel, and azalea. Locally they share the area with other heaths including the fetterbush, the dog-hobble and the Carolina rhododendron. The dog-hobble is the exasperation of the bear hunter and his dogs. The bear can "brute" his way through the tangle of bushes, but dogs and hunter get all hobbled up. The leaves and blossoms of dog-hobble resemble those of fetterbush, but fetterbush is an upright shrub; dog-hobble is low and fernlike.

The Carolina rhododendron, or deer laurel, grows a dense roadside cover between the overlook and Mount Pisgah. Smallest of the native rhododendrons, it is first to bloom, and opens its pink clusters with the white flowers of fetterbush and dog-hobble in May. The mountain laurel, catawba rhododendron, and the azaleas bloom late May into June, followed by rosebay rhododendron in July. July is also the time for Saint-John's-wort, a heathlike shrub that lines a robust fringe of copper-yellow along the nearby motor road. The name hearkens back to medieval Europe and means St. John's plant. A species native to Europe was hung over the doorway on St. John's Day to keep evil spirits from entering at night.

Many native plants are named for plants they resembled in the homelands of our European forefathers. The heath family is named for one of its group, the heather of the Scottish Highlands.

The heaths of the Southern Highlands are the ancestors of many ornamental shrubs that delight the green thumbs of suburbia. In the mountains the heaths and other attractive plants often go by a name unfamiliar in the horticulture catalogues. The mountain name breathes folklore. The name used by the landscape architect and the suburban gardener frequently borrows from mythology, or honors a famous botanist: *fetterbush*-Pieris, a Greek muse; *dog-hobble*-Leucothoe, a Babylonian princess; *white laurel*-rosebay rhododendron, Greek for "rose tree"; *red laurel*-catawba rhododendron; *deer laurel*-Carolina rhododendron; *minniebush*-Menziesia, in honor of Archibald Menzies, botanist; *honeysuckle*-azalea, Greek for "dry"; and *ivy*-mountain laurel (resembles the Greek laurel).

The **Devil's Courthouse Tunnel** is 721 feet long.
422.1 miles.

View of Devil's Courthouse
422.4 miles
elev. 5,462

The courthouse is a bare rock summit, rugged in profile and deserving its association with the Devil. There are many "devilish" features in the Highlands, including a Devil's Backbone, Devil's Staircase, Devil's Peephole, and Devil's Garden. All are rocky and rugged.

Like a conventional courthouse, this Devil's abode has its legal chambers. Within the rocky innards is a cave where legend claims the devil still holds court. Venturesome souls have entered this dismal inner sanctum, but fortunately the court was never in session. At least no one claims the unearthly experience of witnessing the Devil preside over his assembled demons.

In Cherokee folklore the courthouse was the private dancing chambers of a semi-heroic, semi-ridiculous Devil of their own creation, the slant-eyed giant Judaculla. Here he entertained his friends and also secluded himself.

Between the parking overlook and the tunnel, a trail inclines gradually up to the rock summit. It has been marked as a nature trail, with easels bearing plant descriptions. The forest along the way is a vigorous young growth of spruce and balsam with a spindly yet flourishing understory of catawba rhododendron snaking up fifteen or more feet before it branches. The leaves are unusually long and in marked contrast to the dwarfed and wind-buffeted specimens of the same shrub growing on the exposed crown of the courthouse.

Beneath the conifers, the large pliant leaves are best adapted to glean every possible speck of sunlight filtering through the dense canopy. On the exposed crest the rhododendron has small, stout leaves, best adapted for withstanding the frequently vicious winds.

The trail enters a rocky platform atop the "roof" of the courthouse—a sweeping 360° view into the French Broad, Tuckaseigee, and upper Pigeon River valleys.

Directly below, away from the Parkway, is the abrupt descent of Courthouse Ridge. In the left foreground, a long ridge reaches out from Pisgah Ledge and builds up at its extremity to 5,100-foot Pilot Mountain. This is the *Tsu-wah-tul-dee* of the Cherokee, the home of a mythical village within the mountain where everyone lived a life of song, dancing, and feasting.

In the right foreground Brushy Ridge slants away from the Pilot, rising back to Pisgah Ledge, and builds into a row of three higher mountains, Tanasee Bald, Herrin Knob, and Mount Hardy.

Continuing around on our 360° turn, Fork Ridge forms the dominant crestline, declining gradually from Mount Hardy, and eases into the green basin of Bubbling Creek.

Rising as two surging domes on the opposite side are the round-topped knobs of Little Sam and Big Sam made famous in the Big Fire of 1925. Near at hand, on the right, is spruce-covered Chestnut Knob. The swing is completed with the return to the Pilot.

It is typically mountaineer to attach "big" and "little" to two nearby land features of similar appearance but different size. In the northern section of the Parkway we see a Big Levels and a Little Levels, a Big Spy and a Little Spy.

The Sams were probably named for one certain Sam, which Sam is not known. They are believed to be the cattle ranging grounds of Benoni Sams prior to the Civil War, when another Sam, a confederate deserter known as Sam Massie, hid out on the mountains.

Another pair of Sams is also involved, one a hunter named Sam Reece, and a wary bruin. The bear frustrated the hunter's attempts to trap him and thus became an obsession: ''I'm a-goin' to get that thar b'ar.'' But Sam's bear wouldn't oblige. He ''refuged hisself up thar on the Knob,'' and tried to be a live problem rather than a dead carcass. After a while folks ceased calling him ''Sam's Bear.'' They just referred to him as Sam.

View of Mount Hardy (Black Mountain)
422.8 miles
elev. 5,415

Fraser fir   mountain ash
northern red oak   red spruce
yellow birch

Mount Hardy honors Dr. James F. E. Hardy, an Asheville physician who earned his city's gratitude during the Civil War.

The mountain rises in front left, across the bowl-like valley of Bubbling Spring Branch.

Much of the original dark green spruce and balsam were burned off in the Big Fire of 1925. Eventually they will reclaim the slopes, but only after a long recovery period. Beech, buckeye, and birch are slowly replacing the pin cherry and mountain ash, and preparing the way.

NORTHERN RED OAK

In 1942 the North Carolina Division of the United Daughters of the Confederacy established a memorial forest on Mt. Hardy to honor the 125,000 North Carolina veterans of the Civil War.

During the years 1854-60, the man known as the father of the U.S. Weather Bureau, Arnold Guyot, camped in the southern ranges, making measurements of the outstanding peaks. His methods were very thorough and he used the most advanced techniques then known in his native Switzerland.

Guyot came to America in 1848 at the invitation of the great scientist, Louis Agassiz, and taught geology for many years at Princeton University. He soon became interested in mapping and measuring the Appalachians.

Mt. Guyot, 4,580 feet, in New Hampshire, and Mt. Guyot, 6,621 feet, in the Smokies, reveal the extent of his travels.

In 1858 he measured Mt. Hardy. His reading by aneroid barometer of 6,275 feet is remarkably close to the 6,100 feet presently determined with instruments more reliable than those of Guyot's day.

Beech Gap
423.2 miles
elev. 5,340

Exit N.C. 1368 to Rosman 20 miles south, N.C. 1111 to Canton and I-40, 25 miles north.

The gap is a small ''levels'' atop Pisgah Ledge. In the high regions of the southern Appalachians, ''levels'' and ''benches'' frequently cover extensive areas at or near the crest-line. Oddly enough, they are often more subject to wind violence than the nearby peaks. Their sturdy cover

BEECH

of beech, birch, buckeye, and northern red oak is best adapted to conditions too severe for the spruce and balsam. Beeches predominate in the gap. Sturdy and squat, they stay put in spite of the biggest "wind-blow."

Lightning, a despoiler of many highland trees, seldom slashes the beech. Reputedly the oil throughout the tree repels electricity. This oil is richly contained in the abundant nut crop each autumn and makes a delicious feast for bear, turkey, grouse, squirrel, fox, deer, raccoon, and 'possum.

The beech has leaves of near perfect symmetry. Light beneath, dark above, they are a two-tone green contrasting against smooth, gray branches. The leaves stay on, crinkled and golden brown, well into winter.

While generally robust, beech is very sensitive to fire and frost. Many local beeches were seared by the Big Fire of 1925 even though it didn't burn over the gap. The beech is one of the last trees to leaf out in spring. Those in the gap are not in full leaf until mid-June.

View from the Head of Courthouse Valley
423.5 miles
elev. 5,362

The view down Courthouse Creek is similar to the eastward sweep from Devil's Courthouse. The forested foothills gradually level into broad flatlands of the French Broad River. Beyond it in the mist-rimmed distance rises the Blue Ridge. Tanasee Ridge extends on the far right like an irregular chain joining the Blue Ridge and Pisgah Ledge.

The French Broad forms from streams rising in the great bowl outlined by all three ranges and flows in a hungry, evergrowing crescent through the entire central highlands into the Tennessee River.

The upper French Broad Valley is one of the most fertile sections in America and grows bumper crops of corn, fruits, and vegetables. Many fields are bright through the entire summer with lavish gladiolus.

Centuries ago, in 1540, when the valley was a broad wilderness with no more than an occasional Indian village, the Spanish conquistador, Hernando De Soto, came northward from Florida in search of gold. He had been second in command under Pizarro in the sack of Peru and now sought to find great wealth on his own.

With an army of several hundred men, De Soto moved through present Georgia up the Savannah River and crossed the Blue Ridge somewhere along the far skyline. He found an Indian village but no gold, and pushed westward where he died of fever on the banks of the Mississippi. The remnant of his army, greatly reduced by warfare, reached the safety of Mexico in 1543.

View of Tanasee Bald
423.7 miles
elev. 5,380

Seen from the Parkway, the mountain is a swell rising from the levels of Beech Gap. The cap of spruce and balsam shows that it reaches into a "Canadian" climate. Old-timers remember it as a parklike campsite blessed with a spring nearly on the mountain top. Grazing helped to keep back the forest.

The word Tanasee is derived from the Cherokee *Tanasi,* the name of an Indian village below the southern slopes of the mountain at or near the mouth of Tanasee Creek. The meaning has been lost to the present generation but the name of "Tennessee" is very much with us.

Tanasee Creek flows down the Bald into the Tuckaseigee River, which moves north along the Balsam and Smoky Mountains into the Little Tennessee. This river rolls into the Volunteer State and joins the big Tennessee a short distance below Knoxville before going on to the Mississippi and the Gulf of Mexico.

Tanasee Bald figures prominently in Cherokee folklore as *Tsu-ne-gun-yi,* the home of the mythical, slant-eyed giant *Tsul-kalu.* The name is generally pronounced in our language as Judaculla. On the south side of the mountain, away from the Parkway, is a grassy bald said to have been cleared by Tsul-kalu for his farm. His clearing is still in evidence although it is being filled in by trees and shrubs.

H. C. Wilburn, chronicler of Cherokee lore, believes that the true "Judaculla Old Fields" are located near mile 431, high on Richland Balsam. Perhaps the mythical Judaculla, or Tsul-kalu, had two farms.

The explanation of the grassy fields near the summits of high mountains has eluded many naturalists and historians. Indians are believed to be the probable cause. In the lowlands they often set fires to drive out game. In the mountains they burned off the timber to create grass clearings for deer and elk.

Tanasee Bald, however, was the mythical handiwork of Tsul-kalu.

Many stories are told about this supernatural owner of all the game in the mountains. One oft-told tale describes his courtship with a Cherokee girl of old Kanuga town on the banks of the Pigeon.

The girl was of marriageable age and her mother cautioned her to take care and choose someone who would be a good provider. The mother slept in the house while the girl slept outside in a small lodge. One dark night Tsul-kalu came and asked the girl if he could court her. "I am a great hunter," he told her. "I own all the game in the mountains."

She could not see the giant in the dark but his assurances convinced her and she agreed. Just before dawn he left. In the morning the girl went out and found a slain deer. This pleased her mother and they had deer steaks together.

Tsul-kalu came many nights but always stole away before dawn. Each time he brought deer or other game. The mother was content that her daughter had married a good provider but she became curious to see her son-in-law. Tsul-kalu was sensitive about his appearance and the girl was barely able to persuade him. He warned that her mother must not say that he looked frightful, *Usga-se-ti-yu*.

The next morning he remained in the lodge and the girl told her mother to look in. She took one look at the slant-eyed giant lying doubled up on the floor, his toes scraping the roof and his head among the rafters, and ran into the house screaming, "Usga-se-ti-yu! Usga-se-ti-yu!"

The humiliated giant fled from the village and did not return for several days. Then one night he came for his wife and took her to his home on Tsu-ne-gun-yi, and never returned again to Kanuga.

Many times people from Kanuga would hear the giant dancing with his friends within the rocky chambers by Tsu-ne-gun-yi. But none of them ever saw him again.

View of Herrin Knob
424.4 miles
elev. 5,510

Herrin Knob rises near at hand, on the left. Beyond, Tanasee Ridge leads from Tanasee Bald and reaches into the misty miles to join the Blue Ridge on the horizon. Tanasee Ridge forms the watershed divide between the French Broad and the Tuckaseigee Rivers. In the distant straightaway, Toxaway Mountain is recognized by its high, level crest line. To the right is the scalloped profile of Whiteside Mountain.

The name Herrin Knob gives evidence that phonetics and spelling do not always see eye to eye. "The incorrect spelling of this mountain was called to my attention by Mrs. Henry B. Foy, Waynesville, N.C. Mrs. Foy is the daughter of James Pickney Herren. It was for Mr. Herren the mountain was named. Mr. Herren owned approximately one thousand acres in this vicinity and operated a sawmill at the base of the mountain." *(Garrett Smathers, Park Naturalist, 1954)*

Tuckaseigee lakes, a group of three on the headwaters, can be partly seen about five miles down the valley.

Mount Hardy Gap
424.2 miles
elev. 5,490

The low dip on the great Balsam range between Mount Hardy and Herrin Knob. A foot trail, part of the network covering the National Forest, extends between the mountains. Most gaps on the rugged crest of the Pisgah Ledge and the Balsams have never served for other than foot trail crossings. The terrain is too severe for roads. These foot trails have seen constant use by generations of woodsmen.

View of Wolf Mountain
424.8 miles
elev. 5,550

A head-on view down the crest line of Wolf Mountain descending into the Tuckaseigee Valley. Wolf Lake forms at its base.

The broken country below was a final retreat for the wolf packs. During the Civil War they were given a respite from hunting pressure and became numerous in the remoter regions. With return of peace among his own kind, man resumed his warfare against the wolf.

Hunters wise in the habits of the wolf tracked relentlessly for the bounty and the pelt. As the wolves decreased, the hunters deplored seeing their "money crop" disappear. One hunter tracked a she-wolf to her den and killed her litter of pups. He delivered them to the county courthouse and collected his bounty. "Didn't you get the old she-wolf?" "Nope, I left her up thar to raise me another litter. Warn't no sense in killin' my milch cow."

TIMBER WOLF

Local farmers and herdsmen gunned the wolf out of existence in spite of the reluctant bounty hunters. They wanted safe pastures for their livestock. Wolves were exterminated in the early 1900s.

Below in the foothills the smooth, irregular patches in the forest mark the upland pastures where herds of Angus and Herefords graze and fatten. And never the howl of a wolf.

Wolf Bald
425.3 miles

A high point on the Balsam Range at the head of Wolf Bald Mountain.

Buckeye Gap
425.5 miles
elev. 5,377

The yellow buckeye is among the first "mountain top" hardwoods to leaf out in spring. Likewise it is the first to lose its leaves. They show their peachlike tints of red and yellow and fall away by August or early autumn.

The buckeye is generally found along river banks or in moist coves, but is lured to these mountain tops by heavy rainfall. It occurs rarely, if at all, along the Parkway north of Blowing Rock, probably because of dryer soil.

YELLOW BUCKEYE

In spring, soon after the palmate leaves unfold, the tree is brightened with blossoms of candle-light yellow. In summer they develop into loose bunches of smooth, leathery fruits about the size of a golf ball containing two shiny brown buckeyes. Folks carry them in their pockets for luck, a custom from southern Europe where horse chestnuts are still carried to ward off rheumatism.

The raw buckeyes are poisonous, although Indians found roasting made them eatable. Few wild animals will eat them except the mountain boomer, or red squirrel.

The wood is light, strong, and easily worked. Old mountain homes still have bread trays and utensils carved from buckeye.

Horsebone Gap
elev. 5,260
red oak
yellow birch

Uncle Newt viewed the Tuckaseigee Valley for awhile, then he turned around and remarked, "Talkin' about names, this here gap's got a good'un. This ole horse just plumb give out and died in this here gap. His bones hung around fur a right smart while, though, and folks commenced to callin' er Horsebone Gap."

Haywood Gap
426.5 miles
elev. 5,225

A foot trail crosses the Balsams between Haywood County on the northeast and Jackson County on the southwest. The folks of long ago, or "old people," in Jackson

County went across the Balsams to Haywood through Haywood Gap. The name has clearly come from their side of the mountain. People in Haywood County may have referred to the crossing as Jackson Gap. Natural features were often known by different names by the people living on opposite sides of the large mountain ranges.

Rough Butt Bald
427.1 miles

Rough Butt Bald butts up on the near right. "Butt" is a term describing a mountain that "butts off," or breaks abruptly downward. "Butt" Uncle Newt calls by a different tune. "Ever had someone say he'd like to kick you in the pants? Well, this here Butt has a callin' likeness."

Bear Pen Gap
427.6 miles
elev. 5,560
trail

View down Piney Mountain Creek into Tuckaseigee Valley.

Bear trails usually cross the mountains through a gap. Olden time bear hunters built their bear pens in the gaps to have the advantage of level ground. The bear pen is a deadfall of locust logs.

Lured by such tasty morsels as a bull's head or a hambone, the bear pulls the bait and triggers the deadfall.

Bear Trap Gap
428.5 miles
elev. 5,580

bears along the Parkway

The Gap is at the head of Bear Trap Ridge slanting off to the east. A bear trap has a massive pair of steel jaws armed with piercing steel teeth. Unlike a bear pen, which was generally built in a gap, the traps were laid along a bear trail according to the judgment of the hunter. A heavy chain with a grapnel at one end was secured to the trap and prevented the bear from dragging it any great distance. The steel claws of the grapnel clawed into rocks and trees like an anchor.

Bear Trail Ridge
430.4 miles
elev. 5,865

BLACK BEAR

The ridge descends from the Balsam crest toward the west fork of the Pigeon. The three miles of the Balsams between Bear Pen Gap and Bear Trail Ridge are remarkable for the number of mountains, streams, and hollows named for the bear. The U.S. Geological Survey maps of the area show a total of ten.

The names of Bear Wallow Creek, Bear Trail Ridge, and Bear Pen Gap were given by generations of bear hunters who have tromped the steep forests of the Balsams.

One of the greatest bear hunters of the Balsams was hardy, talkative Israel "Wid" Medford. No record is available of his total kills, but they probably registered around the hundred mark. Wid lived a few miles north of Bear Trail Ridge at the foot of Licklog Ridge. He knew the Balsams' every landmark and was often in demand as a guide.

His fellow hunters enjoyed Wid's flow of words and salty comments, particularly when resting at night around the campfire. Once, during a hunt in the 1880s, he was asked what he would do if he could live his life over again.

"I'd git me a neat woman," said Wid, "and go to the wildest kentry in creation, an' hunt from the day I was big nuff to tote a rifle gun, ontil ole age an' roomaticks fastened on me."

Cowee Mountains Overlook
430.7 miles
elev. 5,960

The Cowee Mountains are poetic Cherokee. They rise far and straight away, beyond the Tuckaseigee valley. The mountains are named for a once-important Cherokee settlement on the yonder side of the range. The Indians knew it as *Ka-wi,* an abbreviated form of "Place of the Deer Clan."

Haywood-Jackson Parking Overlook
431 miles
elev. 6,020
self-guide loop trail over Richland Balsam, 1.5 mi.

yellow birch *red elder*
pin cherry *blackberry*
mountain ash *hobblebush*
catawba *viburnum*
 rhododendron

The Great Balsam range forms a boundary between Haywood and Jackson Counties. At this place the Balsam crest line is narrow, and contrasting panoramas are seen with a turn of your head. Beyond lie the uplands of Haywood. Behind are the mountain-walled valleys of Jackson.

In the Haywood view, the high barrier of Shining Rock Wilderness reaches from Pisgah Ledge on the right. A slight elevation on the crest line, dead ahead, locates the outcrop of white quartz known as Shining Rock. From our distance of six or so airline miles, the outcrop seldom catches the eye unless focused in a reflective sunbeam. Then it gives bright reason for its name. Quartz outcrops occur over many portions of the mountain.

Shining Rock was a landmark well known to the lumberjacks of the Suncrest Lumber Company. The train hauling logs to the sawmill chugged slowly by Shining Rock on the first leg of its gradual descent to the mill. Logs were carried many lateral miles, back and forth, to descend the vertical mile into the valley and the final levels along the Pigeon's West Fork.

Richland Balsam
431.4 miles
elev. 6,410

This is the high peak of the Great Balsam Range. At this overlook the Parkway attains its high point of 6,053 feet above sea level. A self-guiding nature trail threads the black, spongy soil of Richland Balsam, asking questions and giving answers. How rich is the forest? How old is the mountain? Tall, straight spires of Fraser fir and red spruce grow close together on a mossy forest floor. High altitude creates the same cool, moist environment found in Canada, a thousand miles north. At one time, forests like this covered ten times the area they do now in the Southern Appalachians. Now only a few precious remnants remain. "Rich" is an oft-repeated mountain name and generally refers to the soil. Richland Balsam, a short form of Rich-

RED SPRUCE

Richland Balsam from Cowee Mountains Overlook

land Mountain of the Balsams, gets its name from the stream on its northeast slopes, Richland Creek.

On this mountain the Parkway passes through the edge of Judaculla Old Fields, a grassy bald where the mythical giant of Cherokee folklore raised his corn and beans.

FRASER FIR

The figures 6,245 were chiseled on a rock atop Richland Balsam by a Waynesville friend and fellow scientist of Arnold Guyot to mark the elevation Guyot determined by aneroid barometer.

The Balsam Wooly Aphid—What It Has Wrought

The Balsam Mountains are aptly named for the abundant and beautiful presence of the Fraser fir, or she-balsam. But this beauty is being erased by the ravages of the balsam woolly aphid, a tiny, wingless, sap-sucking insect. A desolate mantle of dead Fraser fir covers the high ridges. Dying trees, like bright torches of yellow or rust, flare among the still living remnant.

The woolly aphid is a native of Europe that appeared in eastern America about 1900. It was first observed in the Southern Highlands in 1956, presumably from infected nursery stock. European fir trees are resistant to infestation and support large aphid populations without serious harm. Native trees show little resistance. The die-off on a visual basis among mature trees seems to be approaching one hundred percent. The feeding aphid injects a substance into the tree that results in obstructing the conduction of water and nutrients.

Woolly aphids produce a dense mass of white, wool-like material that clings to the trunk and branches of the tree. Two to three entirely female generations are produced yearly. Eggs are deposited in the wool and hatch into ''crawlers'' that search out a feeding place on the tree and then stay put. The insects are incapable of directed movement thereafter, and complete their life cycle at this site unless they are distributed by some means other than their own. One frequent means is the wind that carries them airborne on tufts of wool to a chance landing on another Fraser fir. Eggs from the fall generation overwinter on the trees and hatch the following spring.

There are no known insect predators that feed primarily on the woolly aphid. It is hoped that the genetic resources of the Fraser fir can produce a successful survivor. Or, it is hoped, the genetic resources of the woolly aphid will produce a progeny more compatible with its host.

Lone Bald
432.7 miles
elev. 5,625

Lone Bald stands on the near right. Years ago a he-balsam, or red spruce, stood like a sentinel in a grassy bald high on what was formerly known as Lone Balsam Mountain. Then one day the tree fell, and lo, Lone Bald was born.

The name remains but the open grassland has slowly evolved into a cover of squat, wind-rounded shrubs and deciduous trees, stippled with occasional spires of spruce.

Locust Gap
433.3 miles
elev. 5,580
view of Hazelwood

BLACK LOCUST

"There never was no locust a'growin' this fur up the mountain," said Uncle Newt. "No way to my knowin's how this place come to get called Locust Gap. I figure them lumber fellers might of had some need fur locust posts and had a pile of'm settin' out here."

Uncle Newt looked up sharply as a new thought gave a wise look to his eye. "It could be fur one of them bear hunters haulin' locusts up here fur his bear pens. They made'm a kind of deadfall out of locust logs."

Black locust is one of the hardest native woods. Its durability and rot resistance make it unbeatable for fence posts and wooden pegs. Formerly it was used to construct bear pens. A locust pen will last a half century.

The tree blooms in late May to early June, hung with loose white clusters. According to an old mountain saying, a good locust bloom means a poor crop year.

Long Swag
433.7 miles
elev. 5,600

The Long Swag is a shallow depression on the Balsam crest line extending nearly a mile between Locust Gap and Old Bald.

An old trail, later known as the Long Swag road, came from Waynesville and crossed the mountains into the Tuckaseigee Valley. Following the Indian treaties of 1818-19 opening up the upper Tuckaseigee to settlement, many people moved overland by the Long Swag.

By the 1880s, a "dug" road was built to reach a copper mine on the west side below Old Bald. The mine has long been abandoned, but its memory lingers in the cascading waters of Coppermine Creek.

Racking Horse Gap
434.8 miles
elev. 5,400
no parking permitted

"The way I have it is that some fellow pastured a horse up here that was noted for its racking gait." *(H. C. Wilburn, Waynesville, N.C., 1954)*

A racking gait is a fast, high-stepping trot displayed by the skilled equestrians of the English style of horsemanship. If the racking horse ever practiced his talents in these parts, the native nags must have pricked up their ears and snorted.

Doubletop Mountain seen from Flat Gap
435.3 miles
elev. 5,365

Flat Gap is a miniature "levels" on the Balsam crest line. It makes an appropriate campsite and was used as such by saw-loggers of the early 1900s.

Below the gap is the young valley of Deep Ridge Creek sliding down between the long reach of Snaggy Bald Ridge on the left and Dark Ridge Opposite. The stream feeds into the Tuckaseigee, a hurrying river that gathers waters from the Great Balsams and the Cowee range on the far horizon.

The Cherokee village of Tuckaseigee, *Tsi-ksi-tsi,* once stood on the river banks below. It was destroyed by a hundred and fifty mounted whites under John Sevier in 1781 when the Cherokee were allies of the British. The name is said to mean "terrapin place," in reference to the slow creepy current of the river at the village site.

The Cherokee of that day had no written language. Accordingly, their speech varied from generation to generation. Original meanings often became obscured. Grandchildren were said to have difficulty understanding their grandparents.

In 1821, Sequoyah, a scholarly Cherokee, devised a phonetic alphabet, or syllabary, to write and perpetuate the language and history of his people.

Licklog Gap
435.7 miles
elev. 5,365
view of Water-rock Knob

Licklog Gap is a place where cattle liked to gather. Here the herders kept them supplied with salt contained in holes or "boxes" cut into a "licklog."

Locally the highlands could be appropriately known as the Glade Mountains, for the grassy glades spread among the forest. For years these shady mountain meadows had been pastured prior to becoming part of the national forest. Spring through fall, loose herds of free ranging cattle, swine, horses, and sheep grazed the uplands. They fed on the grassy balds and helped to keep them open by eating the shrubs and young trees.

The Great Balsam Mountains are named for the heavy "mane" of red spruce, he-balsam, and Fraser fir, she-balsam, that formerly covered its crest. This forest has been largely logged off or consumed by fires. Only a sentinel-few of these hardy evergreens poke up from isolated high spots.

View of
Grassy Ridge Mine
436.8 miles
elev. 5,250

A pile of 'diggin's' below the overlook locates a mica mine operated on the slopes of Grassy Ridge at various times, including the World War II years. After the war the price of mica dropped, resulting in closure of the mine.

A more lasting feature is the elemental drama of trees and weather. The forest cover is an "orchard" of northern red oak extending up the sides of Steestatchee Bald on the near right. The trees rise in thin ranks above a grassy ground cover. Their rounded profiles and blunted stature resemble old apple trees in an abandoned orchard. The trees derive vigor from the rich soil, but the vigor is dedicated to survival more than growth. The physical onslaught of savage weather weeds out an annual toll of trees. But the survivors manage to touch each others' branches and shade Steestachee to the summit.

Life and death stand side by side. Gray-slick limbs of dead trees reveal the lethal power of wind and ice.

View of
Steestachee Bald
439 miles
elev. 4,780
Roadside easel:
American chestnut

Steestachee Bald shows prominently on the near right, a high elevation on the Balsam Range. Steestachee is our pronunciation for what the trained tongue of the Cherokee glibly utters as *tsi-ste-tsi*. In his language it means mouse, also rat, and the lack of accurate facts leave it up to the imagination as to why the mountain has become Steestachee Bald.

According to Cherokee folklore, however, many animals had a special mountain of their own. The bears convened at *Ku-wa-hi,* in the Smokies, where they had their town houses and held dances every fall before retiring for the winter. Their chief was a great white bear.

The Indians knew the Smokies' famed Mt. LeConte as *Wah-lah-see-yah,* the frog place. A giant rabbit is also known to have lived in a high, secluded peak in the Smokies. Perhaps a great mouse of Cherokee lore once dwelled on Steestachee Bald.

DEER MOUSE

The common mice of the mountains are the deer mice, seldom seen by Parkway visitors because of their night wanderings. Their large eyes and ears give them a deerlike appearance, at least for mice. They are busy little animals with thrifty habits. In fall they store amazing quantities of seeds in underground retreats. The Cherokee sometimes searched for their food caches and looked upon the animals as their friends. The mice, no doubt, held a different opinion of the Cherokee.

Cove Field Ridge
439.4 miles
elev. 4,620

A mountain-walled inlet lies between the overlook and Cove Field Ridge. The rural character of farm life has been infiltrated with suburban and retirement homes. The year-round mild climate of the valley lands lures settlers from North and South.

The **Pinnacle Ridge Tunnel** is 895 feet long.
439.7 miles.

Saunook
440.1 miles
elev. 4,375

Pinnacle Ridge extends westward from the Balsam crest, tapering downward for over a mile, and then builds up to a sharp pinnacle, 4,250 feet, overlooking Waynesville. Your view sweeps an impressive experience in mountain scenery: the Plott Balsams, a 6,000-foot range crossing the Great Balsams between Balsam and Soco Gaps.

View of Waynesville
440.9 miles
elev. 4,110

Waynesville and its industrial suburb of Hazelwood are seen in the bottomlands below the long reach of the Plott Balsam range. This is the homeland of the apple, from early Winesap to late Macintosh; from juicy Delicious to long lasting Roman. Orchards terrace the slopes and pattern the valleys.

According to tradition, Waynesville was named for "Mad Anthony" Wayne at the suggestion of Colonel Love, a native soldier who served under him in the Revolutionary War.

The Waynesville community has a homespun holiday air throughout the green and growing seasons. Spring has the festival air of apple blossom time when the orderly

APPLE BLOSSOM

rows of trees pass in review. And the nearby forests echo the mood with a profusion of "wild pretties." Some of the wild pretties have an attraction that reaches beyond the eye. In spring the young at heart and strong of stomach head for the hills and hunt a wild onion called the ramp. Ramps add flavor and a heartburn tang to a skillet-hot mess of eggs and country-cured ham.

RAMP

Summer is a pleasure that drifts from day to day, sparked by special events and square dances. In summer the devotees of the "hog rifle" convene on Fie Top Mountain of the nearby Catalooche Balsams for a target shoot. Some of the ancient flintlocks are so big they must be aimed from a prone position with a support beneath the barrel. The boom that follows the trigger-pull makes the leaves fall.

Autumn brings color spilling over the highlands and brings homefolks and vacationers together for a season's farewell. The solid core residents of Waynesville-Hazelwood are convincing boosters for their community. They like it year-round and lay down the welcome mat. Here is the home of the best: the best orchards, dairies, poultry farms, truck farms, and industries. And the best livin.' "Come and see us," they say, "and stay all day with us."

Rabb Knob Overlook
441.9 miles

Scanning Richland Creek Valley, an inlet of the Pigeon.

Balsam Gap is just down the road a piece. The overlook peers from the throat of this low pass over the Balsams. At 3,370 feet, however, it is higher than many mountains, particularly those of the Blue Ridge.

As may now be apparent, the Indians had a well-developed trail system. Many footpaths were followed by white settlers moving into the Indian homeland. In later years the same trails marked the general route of major highways and railroads.

The first large group of white men came through Balsam Gap in 1776 and spread havoc among the Indians in the Tuckaseigee Valley and beyond the Cowees. General Griffith Rutherford led a force of twenty-four hundred fighting men to punish the hostile Cherokee for raiding the white settlements. The destruction of Indian homes and crops forced the starving survivors to beg for peace. Peace did not last, however. The whites wanted the red man's land and did not cease until it was finally acquired by war and treaty.

Following the red man's defeats, settlers moved through the gap along one of the few wagon roads crossing the Balsams. In the wake of the road builders came the iron horse. In 1883 the Southern Railway laid a track through the gap, at 3,335 feet, the highest standard-gauge crossing in eastern America.

Balsam Gap
443.1 miles
elev. 3,370

Overpasses U.S. 23 and 19A; 12 miles west to Sylva; 8 miles east to Waynesville.

The Orchards
444.6 miles
elev. 3,810

Apple orchards cover the well-drained bottomlands of Richland Creek. Their beauty reflects the vigilance of the orchardist. He worries his crop of blossoms through the spring frosts. He sprays the insect enemies that come with the blooms, and with the button-size fruit. He prunes, he paints, he patches. As the crop matures, he makes supports for the heavy-laden branches. Late summer into fall, his men climb the trees and carefully place the ripe apples into sacks. Hauled to the apple barn, they are sorted for size and quality, and placed in crates and baskets. Trailer trucks haul them to their familiar display on supermarket shelves, red, tasty, and cared-for.

Below and far away the Parkway traces the Great Balsam range from the broad hollow of Balsam Gap to the dark fringe of spruce and fir over Richland Balsam.

Mt. Lynn Lowry
445.2 miles
elev. 6,280

A sixty-foot illuminated cross rises on the mountain top in memoriam to the daughter of Gen. and Mrs. Sumpter L. Lowry who died in 1962, age 15, a victim of leukemia. The cross was dedicated August 9, 1965 by Dr. Billy Graham. ''She dearly loved these mountains.''

Woodfin Cascades
446.7 miles
elev. 4,535

Below the crest of Mt. Lynn Lowry a basinlike depression funnels the drain-off into a shaft of water. Arrow straight, it cascades down the mountainside. The sound of its flow and spray is like the wind—a cool sound enclosed beneath the shade of hemlock and beech. The sound is alive and invigorating, yet as you watch and listen, it drifts into the background of your thoughts and becomes a kind of silence.

View of Fork Ridge
449 miles
elev. 5,280

A gunsight view between Cutoff Ridge and Fork Ridge into Scott Creek Valley: two prongs of Fork Creek join at the foot of Fork Ridge. ''Prong'' and ''fork'' are descriptive names applied to many mountain streams. Their course is swift and straight, and they merge into each other at a sharp angle. Prongs are generally smaller streams and join into forks.

The rock face behind the overlook is a profile of the native gneiss, veined with granite. The gneiss originated from layers of sandstone and shale compressed at a depth of several miles below the earth's surface. The resultant intense pressure formed the gneiss, the foundation rock of the Southern Highlands.

During a later geological period, the gneiss was penetrated, beneath the earth, by molten rock that solidified into granite. During a still later period the region was uplifted into mountains by massive earth movements, and finally exposed to our view by erosion. The Parkway engineers have placed the geological story in sharp focus by means of the rock cut.

View of Yellow Face
450 miles
elev. 5,610

Straight ahead on the Plott Balsam crest line is Yellow Face, the "two-faced" mountain. Settlers in Soco Valley, on the right, knew it as Yellow Face; the early natives in Scott Valley, on the left, knew it as Rocky Face. Either name is appropriate, but Yellow Face was first to reach the map-maker's ear.

The local rock type has a greenish-yellow cast that gives the mountain its sallow complexion. This appearance is enhanced in late summer when the sun dries the soil on the heights of Yellow Face and the plants become withered and sere.

View from Waterrock Knob
6,292 feet
451.2 miles
elev. 5,718

A cool flow of spring water pours over the edge of "camp rock," high on the mountain. Generations of hunters, herders, and lumbermen have rested and quenched their thirst by the Waterrock.

Waterrock Knob marks the joining of the Plott Balsams and the Great Balsam ranges. Although represented as the high peak of the Plotts, its location makes it a part of both ranges. As such, the Knob is second only to the 6,410-foot Richland Balsam in height.

The view from Waterrock Knob stretches the eyes over the heart of the Highlands. From a 360° vantage point, you scan the main ranges of the Southern Appalachians.

Viewed across the motor road, the Great Balsams head northwestward into the Great Smokies. Southeast are the long rows of the Cowees and the far off Nantahalas. Well to the southeast, beyond Tanasee Ridge and Pisgah Ledge, rises the vague outline of the Blue Ridge.

CAROLINA JUNCO

Northeast, the Newfound Mountains rise above the Pigeon River Valley. 'Way beyond the southern tip of the Newfounds and the city of Asheville loom the Blacks and the Craggies.

There are many times to enjoy the wide-flung vista from Waterrock, but none better than a summer evening. Clouds are radiantly white, trimmed with fire. The descending sun covers the mountains with a chameleon cloak of changing color. Bright sunshine drifts into bronze that lingers and deepens into purple dusk. The clouds and mountains mingle on the horizon and drift together in the night. A star appears and the last bird sings.

Browning's Knob—North Carolina Remembers
Browning's Knob looms beyond a plaque on Waterrock Knob honoring H. Getty Browning, 1881-1966, location

Waterrock Knob Overlook

and claims engineer and parkway consultant for the North Carolina Highway Commission.

Browning worked tirelessly and with great skill to secure the present Parkway route through North Carolina. The Parkway was authorized as a federal project in 1933 as "a scenic highway connecting the Shenandoah and Smoky Mountains National Parks."

The route through Virginia was agreed to promptly, but the locating of the route from Virginia to the Smokies became a major issue between North Carolina and Tennessee.

Tennesseans proposed a "fair share" route with the northern half passing through North Carolina and the southern half passing through and ending in Tennessee. Browning ably promoted an "all Carolina" route.

Secretary of Interior Harold L. Ickes invited the proponents to a "debate" in Washington, D.C., held September 18, 1934. Each group, including the governors and legislators from each state, had the floor for one hour and fifteen minutes; each group had fifteen minutes for resume and rebuttal. Secretary Ickes served as chairman and timekeeper.

Browning, as North Carolina's chief spokesman, came thoroughly prepared and delivered a masterpiece augmented with visual aids. His cause was by no means assured. An advisory committee previously selected by Ickes recommended the "fair share" route.

Two months of suspense slowly passed. Mr. Ickes reviewed and perused. Then on November 10, 1934, he announced in favor of North Carolina to the huzzas of the Tarheels and the disbelief of the Volunteers. North Carolina gratefully remembers H. Getty Browning.

Cranberry Ridge
452.1 miles
elev. 5,475

The cranberry of the mountains is not the supine, matted shrub of lowland bogs, but an upright shrub that colonizes high slopes and summits. The small, pinkish flower is mostly a central column of stamens protruding from four recurved petals. The dark red berries ripen in August and September and have a sometimes taste. Sometimes they are tasty and tart; othertimes flat and insipid.

View of Woolyback
452.3 miles
elev. 5,420

The low, rounded ridge in the right foreground has a "woolyback" cover of rhododendron and mountain laurel shrubs. Here and there a few spruce poke through.

Near mile 452.7 is a large patch of flame azalea. In bloom, these shrubs are among the world's most brilliant, displaying a range of flaming hues from lemon yellow to deep orange.

The flame azalea is well represented along the Parkway, south of Roanoke, Va. For no apparent reason it is all but nonexistent northward. The bloom appears from early

AZALEA

May to late June according to the elevation. In the higher, cooler climate of Carolina, the flame is weeks behind the bloom peak for the Virginia section of the Parkway. In the azalea patch, many of the shrubs bloom in July.

Other members of this attractive tribe are also found in the mountain forest. The pink azalea is the most wide-spread and is well represented at moderate elevations over the entire Parkway.

View of Hornbuckle Valley
453.4 miles
elev. 5,105

Hornbuckle Creek leads into Soco Valley and the Qualla reservation of the Cherokee. A Cherokee soldier of the Civil War once farmed the land just below. He was sur-vived on the old homestead by several off spring, includ-ing son Israel.

"The creek is named for my father, James Hornbuckle. He died in 1896 at about 60. He served in the Union Army, enlisted in Knoxville, Tennessee, Company D, 3rd Regi-ment under Major W. W. Rollins of Asheville.

"My father was in a skirmish at the close of the war. The Federals came across the Smokies, down through Soco Gap to the Cherokee land. An Indian sergeant held a parlay with some of the outpost Cherokee who were in Confederate uniform. He wanted them to come over to the Union side. They wouldn't. After a skirmish the Union men retreated back through the Gap." *(Israel Hornbuckle, Cherokee, N.C., 1954)*

Most of the Cherokee, about four hundred soldiers, enlisted under their white chief, "Little Will" Thomas, in the Thomas Legion of the Confederate Army, and served mainly as a border guard, protecting the passes leading from Tennessee.

On February 2, 1864, a skirmish occurred between Union forces and the Thomas Legion. The following reports indicate that some of the fighting was done with pen and paper.

"While in Tuckaleechee Cove I received information that the force of Indians and whites commanded by the rebel Thomas (formerly U.S. Indian Agent for the Cherokee Nation) was near the forks of the Little Tennes-see and Tuckaseigee rivers in North Carolina.... I ordered Major Davidson with his regiment... to pursue this force and destroy it.... The enemy were 250 strong. Of these, 22 Indians and 32 whites were captured, includ-ing some officers. It is reported that less than 50 made their escape, the remainder being either killed or wounded... nearly 200 of them having been killed."
(Report of Brig. Gen. S. D. Sturgis, Union Army, Febru-ary 4, 1864)

The Confederate version begs to differ: "... on the second instant they advanced up the Little Tennessee and Tuckaseigee to the mouth of Deep Creek, when the Indians under my command arrested their progress. The enemy lost about 12 killed and wounded, the Indians five. I am informed the northern forces boast of killing 200.'' *(Report of Col. W. H. Thomas, Confederate Army, February 28, 1864)*

Fed Cove
455.1 miles
elev. 4,550

The name Fed Cove is a deception that hints a tale involving a skirmish between the Union "Feds" and the Cherokee Legion of Colonel Will Thomas. The cove probably had its share of angry rifle fire during the Civil War, but only as a part of a lawless land. The Cherokee skirmished with pillaging bushwackers and renegades more than with invading "blue coats." When the Yankees arrived, the war was all but over.

Fed Cove is named for a Mr. Fed, who "had him a cabin thar."

Soco Gap
455.7 miles
elev. 4,340

U.S. 19: Cherokee, 8 miles west; Waynesville, 13 miles east; Asheville, 42 miles east via Maggie Valley; Lake Junaluska, and I-40.

Sa-gwa-hi, or "one place," is the Cherokee name for Soco Creek, heading westward from the gap to the Oconaluftee River. Both the creek and the gap were dubbed Soco by the whites. The evolution of the word is typical of the transition from Indian speech to English. Sagwahi became Socah, and finally Soco.

The gap itself is known to the Cherokee as *ahaluna,* meaning "ambush place," or "where they watched." The name recalls a bloody incident when a large party of invading Shawnees were ambushed and killed save for one warrior. He was released, minus his ears, to take the tidings back to his people.

The incident probably occurred in the mid-1700s after a general Cherokee withdrawal behind the Balsams. The oncoming press of the whites plus the forays of Indian enemies forced the move. Naturally, they maintained an outpost at the gap, as it represented the main entrance into their homeland from both north and east. White fighters generally avoided these well-traveled routes when invading the Cherokees, and thus dodged the fate of the Shawnee war party.

Johnathan Creek Parking Area
456.2 miles
elev. 4,460

red oak
basswood or lynn
black cherry
black locust

eastern hemlock
serviceberry
bracken fern

The pleasant tang of wood smoke wisps from campfires beneath the forest edge. Daytime campers enjoy a sojourn where they can mosey around a bit and enjoy an outdoor meal.

One Johnathan MacPeters, an early settler, had a place twelve miles below where Johnathan Creek joins the Pigeon River. He stayed long enough to leave his first name.

EASTERN OR CANADIAN HEMLOCK

The Qualla Reservation
457.5-469 miles

BASSWOOD OR LYNN

The Parkway views of the Qualla Reservation behold the ancestral heartland of the Cherokee. Their villages dotted the great Tuckaseigee Valley and spread beyond the misty skylines of the Cowee and the Nantahala mountains.

This nation of Indian mountaineers once held parts of present day North and South Carolina, Tennessee, Georgia, and Alabama. They laid claim to hunting grounds covering most of Kentucky, Tennessee, and the southern portion of West Virginia and Virginia.

A series of wars and treaties finally deprived them of all their land by 1838, and removed them to a reservation in what is now Oklahoma. During this final removal along the well-named Trail of Tears, slightly more than a thousand Cherokee refugees hid out in the mountains. They were allowed to return to land purchased for them by their white chief or agent, Will Thomas. This land formed the heart of the present day Qualla Reservation.

Today the Cherokee country, as viewed in Soco Valley, is a rustic community of farmers, merchants, and craftsmen. Soco Falls, a mile below the Plott Balsams Overlook, is the site of many historic councils and debates. Here in 1812 the Shawnee leader, Tecumseh, is said to have pleaded vainly with the Cherokee to join him in a red man's federation against the white settlers. His persuasive oratory could not dispel the cool logic of the Cherokee leader, Junaluska.

Sarvis Gap
457.6 miles
elev. 4,930

SERVICEBERRY

Two large "sarvis," or serviceberry, trees stand in the gap at the underpass of an Indian Service Road. One has a diameter of 18 inches, extremely large for this species. Both trees are now on the decline and give appearance of great age.

This tree of many names—serviceberry, juneberry, sarvis, and shadblow—is the first abundant bloom in spring, covering itself with a flurry of suspended snowflakes. At low elevations they open in March, while those on the mountain tops blossom in May. At this time they stand out in the leafless forest.

Two forms are found in the mountains. The downy serviceberry, of lower elevations, has a slight furry covering on the leaves, particularly in spring. The smooth serviceberry, like those in the gap, has a slick and more heart-shaped leaf. At middle elevations the two appear to mix. The reddish, pea-sized fruit ripens in June. It is edible, but that of the smooth serviceberry is most sweet and juicy. Bears are particularly fond of them. They will reach up and swipe a pawful and then sit down on their haunches to enjoy the treat.

View of the Plott Balsams
457.9 miles
elev. 5,020

The Plott Balsams, a magnificent range crossing the Great Balsams, span the horizon. They have long been associated with the Plotts, a family of hunters and originators of the famous Plott bear hounds.

Johannes Plott came to America from Heidelberg, Germany, in 1750. Several of his grandchildren later took up land on Johnathan Creek, and it is for this generation in particular that the Plott Balsams are named. Hunters by their campfires still relate the exploits of Amos, Enos, and David Plott.

During one memorable hunt a wounded bear took refuge in a large hole. Amos drew his knife and advanced to kill it. He began his thrust, lost his balance and fell into the jaws and claws of the desperate beast. In the short, violent encounter he managed to strike home with his blade but not before the bear chewed and mauled him severely. The left-handed Amos fell with his right side to the bear, enabling use of his knife hand to best advantage. Otherwise Amos might have ended his bear-hunting days in a death embrace.

The Plott family are the originators of a famed breed of canine hunter, the Plott bear hound. The ancestor of this strong and fearless tracker may have come from Germany with Johannes Plott. However, the breed was developed with the rugged Plott Balsams as its proving grounds. The Plott family selected breeding stock from the best hunters in the region, and the bear gave them trial by combat. Dogs unworthy of the name were culled from the hunting packs or eliminated by the bear.

There are no physical standards for the Plott bear hound. You will never find one in a show ring going through the dandified motions of a groomed poodle. A hunting pack may vary in size, color, or conformation. The standards for this breed are courage, keen nose, stamina, and perseverance.

Many hunters place their name and address on the dog's collar. A hunt may last for days. The hunter gives up, but not his dogs. After a night's rest and a good meal, the hunter goes hunting for his dogs. "Anyone seen my bear dogs? I set'm loose over by Jones Knob. They got on to a bear scent and took off a-bayin' up a storm. I ain't seen or heard nary a one all day." This story happens often. 'Most always man and dogs get together again.

Wolf Laurel Gap
458.2 miles
elev. 5,100

Junction of spur to Mile-High Overlook, Balsam Mountain Campground, Heintooga Overlook.

Both the rosebay and Catawba rhododendron, known regionally as "laurel," grow in the forest understory.

By reputation this high mountain recess is a rattlesnake haven and was formerly inhabited by wolves. As recently as 1910 trappers caught a female wolf in the gap and then trapped her pups one by one until they had the entire litter.

ROSEBAY RHODODENDRON

The native wolf of the southern Appalachians died out at least by 1920. Though fearful of people, the wolf was a menace to sheep and swine. Heavy bounties were offered to rid the country of them. Each hunter commonly had to attest that he did not allow adult females to escape while merely turning in males and pups.

At Wolf Laurel Gap the Parkway leaves the main Balsam range and descends Lead-Off ridge toward the Oconaluftee River and the Smokies.

CATAWBA RHODODENDRON

Mollie Gap
0.9 mile (spur)
elev. 5,352

Members of the Cherokee Council met with North Carolina officials to discuss the purchase of land through the reservation for the Parkway. They drove as far as they could and then walked to the land under consideration. Mollie Arneach, the first woman member of the Indian Council, was first to reach the gap. H. Getty Browning, chief location and claims engineer for North Carolina, named it Mollie Gap in her honor.

**Mile-High
Overlook**
1.3 miles (spur)
elev. 5,280

The Mile-High view of Great Smoky Mountains National Park is a name given by the Parkway. It is well established with the residents of nearby Maggie Valley and environs. They often refer to happenings "up at Mile-High." The overlook is at the head of Pleasant Ridge, a name that carries a left-handed sort of humor. In the days before the establishment of the Park it was anything but pleasant to clamber after cattle grazing on the ridge.

"We'd take our lunch and spend the day herding cattle and the night fox hunting.... Listen at'm run all night. They'd change counties with you.... We'd build us a fire and set around.... The grays would run around in a short circle. When the dogs took off on a long one, you knew they was after a red." *(Jim Plott, Maggie, N.C. 1954)*

RED FOX

Over the Parkway, the way to the Mile-High view is no longer an arduous climb to the mountaintop. Within a "cineramic survey" are the Smokies and the Balsams, two great ranges of the Appalachians.

Of the high horizon peaks, Clingman's Dome is on the far left. At left center Mt. LeConte shows behind the closer profile of Mt. Kephart. A bit right of center is Mt. Guyot. All the middle distance comprises the jagged serrations of the "Sawtooth."

Filling the right span are the Balsams, heading more or less directly into the Smokies. Below, in the middle distance, slightly leftward, is a conspicuously grass-green valley, Big Cove, a remote settlement of the Cherokee Qualla Reservation.

**View of
Maggie Valley**
1.4 miles (spur)
elev. 5,220

The valley is a cool summer retreat along Johnathan Creek. Mountain coolness descends each evening from the bordering ranges. The valley itself averages 3,000 feet above the sea, but lies more than half a mile lower than the hulking Cataloochee and Plott Balsam ranges.

The valley took the homespun name of Maggie in the early 1900s when local sawmill men wanted a post office nearer than the one at Plott, a few miles down the road.

RAVEN

Jack Setzer wrote to the Third Assistant Postmaster General, who replied that the government would establish one if Mr. Setzer carried the mail six months to "show us that you need it."

"After six months, the postmaster said we could have a post office and asked me to send in some names. I sent a bunch but they were all turned down and he asked me to send in some more. I sent in my two girls names, Cora and Maggie; and Venus, and possibly a few others. The postmaster wrote back that Maggie was accepted." *(Jack Setzer, Maggie, N.C. 1954)*

**View of
Lake Junaluska**
2.3 miles (spur)
elev. 5,034

Lake Junaluska honors a Cherokee warrior who fought for and against the white man. Young Junaluska fought in the losing effort to drive out the white invader. He and his people tried to keep an honorable peace and became the allies of the United States in the War of 1812.

Junaluska won the gratitude of Andrew Jackson in Alabama at the Battle of Horseshoe Bend. The fighting against the Creek Indians, fierce allies of the British, was stubborn and bloody. The Creeks fought with desperation from their barricade on a horseshoe bend of the Tallaposa River. Tennessee militia stormed the crude fortification but were driven back.

Junaluska, stationed across the river behind the Creek, observed a group of canoes hidden on the enemy side. He and several of his braves swam the river and towed them to the main body of Cherokee waiting on the river bank. Swiftly they leaped into the canoes and crossed the stream to attack the Creek from the rear. The diversion brought defeat and massacre to the enemy.

Andrew Jackson moved on to New Orleans and greater military fame. He became the seventh President of the United States. At Horseshoe Bend, in 1814, the General pledged his gratitude to Junaluska. But even a president may be denied the right to honor his word. During his administration, Jackson signed away the rights of the Cherokee to remain in their mountain homeland.

**Horse Trough
Ridge**
3.3 miles (spur)
elev. 4,496

Enter Great Smoky Mountains National Park.

In the 1880s a cattle herder from Jonathan Creek observed a hollow basswood nearby and proceeded to fell and hew out two feed troughs. He intended to return with a team and "skin," or haul, them out, but evidently never found time. They lay beside the trail within view of the passersby and finally rotted away.

Black Camp Gap
3.6 miles (spur)

Prior to the Civil War various land owners in the vicinity maintained a cabin in the gap for use when cattle-ranging or hunting. During a forest fire the cabin was scorched but not destroyed. Afterwards, people camping there became blackened from contact with the charred walls.

Blue Ridge Farm

TURKEY VULTURE OR BUZZARD

Six miles further on this paved Park Service road is Balsam Mountain Campground, highest (elev. 5,340) to be reached by auto in the Great Smoky Mountains National Park, with improved trailer and camp space, no permit required, but strictly limited to campground capacity. Next nearest campground is near the Oconaluftee ranger station at end of Parkway on U.S. 441.

Heintooga Picnic Area Overlook
37 sites
end of spur

40 campsites; 100-person capacity; campfire circle; Balsam Mountain Campground.

Two choice scenic spots near Balsam Mountain Campground are the glade of Flat Creek, ending in a waterfall, and Heintooga Overlook, which sweeps the skyline of the higher Smokies range—perhaps forty miles of the entire seventy.

Lickstone Ridge Tunnel
406 feet

Lickstone Ridge
458.9 miles
elev. 5,150

"Lickstone Ridge is a broad flat-top mountain suitable for the purpose that gave rise to its name. The very name itself conjures up stories of a vocation long prevalent in these mountainous sections. In the days when there were no roads except winding trails that could be walked or ridden on horseback, many nights were spent around campfires by neighborhood groups, which carried in salt and two or three days' supply of rations. Salt was spread on a smooth stone if one were available, and the place became a "lickstone." A smooth place on the ground might serve, in which case it was simply a "lick" prefaced by the name of some person whose cattle used it most. In other cases "boxes" were chopped out in the top of a log, and salt poured in. This gave rise to the name "licklog." There are many licklog gaps in the mountains. If the cattle were not already in the vicinity of the "lick" for their periodic "salting," two whoops and three halloas usually brought them bellowing and stampeding." *(H. C. Wilburn, Waynesville, N.C., 1954)*

Bunches Bald Tunnel
290 feet
459.3 miles

View of Bunches Bald
459.5 miles
elev. 4,925

The name of Bunche is applied to a stream, and to a gap and a mountain located on its headwaters. It is likely that Bunche was a lumberman operating in the vicinity before it became part of Great Smoky Mountains National Park.

The Cherokee call the creek *day-u-nisi,* their name for the whirligig beetle. As it does in so many of our ponds and streams, the whirligig beetle lives in sociable swarms throughout the length of the creek. The dark, metallic bodies gleam as they trace a constant series of rapid curves upon the water.

In Cherokee folklore the little water beetle is responsible for starting the earth to grow. Long ago before the earth was created, all was water and all the creatures lived high above in *Gal-un-lati.* It was very crowded and they wanted more room. They wondered what was below the water, and at last *Dayunisi,* "beaver's grandchild," the little water beetle, offered to find out. It dived to the bottom and came up with some soft mud. The mud grew and grew on every side until it became the island we call Earth. Later it was fastened to the sky with four cords, one for each of the cardinal points, but no one remembers who did this.

Bunches Gap
459.7 miles
elev. 4,850

A low point along the crest midway between Sarvis Gap and Big Witch Gap. An Indian Service road extends through all three points. Developed by Civilian Conservation Corps, it was suitable for auto traffic during the late 1940s, and connects the high mountain country with the Soco Valley.

View of
Jenkins Ridge
460.8 miles
elev. 4,445

Jonas Jenkins, a white man, lived by Jenkins Creek on the far side of the big ridge to the left that bears his name. Old men of the Cherokee reservation remember playing with Jenkins's red-headed son back in their boyhood days. *(Arsine Thomas, Cherokee, N.C., 1954)*

The Story of Big Witch

Big Witch Tunnel
353 feet
461.2 miles

Big Witch Gap
461.6 miles
elev. 4,150

The valley home of Big Witch stretches toward Soco Creek, across from the parking overlook. Big Witch, *Tskil-e-gwa,* was the last of the Cherokee eagle killers. He died in 1898, a wizened old man over ninety. The eagle killer was a man designated by the tribe to kill the sacred eagles to obtain feathers for dances and festivals. Only the professional eagle killer who was skilled in the practice and prescribed methods was authorized to kill this great bird.

Big Witch also acquired a reputation among his people as one who made cures and medicine from plants. He hunted for them barefoot, in fair weather or when the snow was knee deep. The Cherokee had profound faith in his ability to cure rheumatism. This barefoot herb doctor must have used his own medicine.

In Indian plant-lore the "sign," or appearance and characteristics of a plant, indicated its use. The fern was used to combat rheumatism because the tightly coiled young fronds, or leaves, unroll and straighten as the plant develops to full size. Medicine made from the fern will, therefore, enable the hunched rheumatic sufferer to stand erect.

LADY FERN

Old or deformed plants were also believed to have great curative powers, such as a tree struck by lightning or a plant with a grotesque parasite growth. A ritual surrounded gathering and giving the medicine. When Big Witch doctored a patient, a large part of the cure lay in the patient's belief that the chants and mysterious motions of his medicine man were frightening off the illness.

Big Witch is a logical name for a medicine man, but it actually has nothing to do with his mastery of cures. *Tse-kill-e-gwa* was first applied to a white man with large, owl-like eyes, who lived as the Cherokee's neighbor on the same clearing. After the white man left, the Indians passed the name on to the medicine man.

sourwood	*red oak*
red maple	*chestnut oak*
black locust	*silverbell*
pignut	

SOURWOOD

The Thomas Divide is the high ridge on the left forming background for the Oconaluftee River Valley and the Qualla Reservation of the Cherokee. Will Thomas, 1805-1893, known to the Cherokee as Will Usdi, or Little Will, lived most of his life with and for the Cherokee. He commenced his career as an Indian trader at the age of twelve managing a post on Soco Creek.

Thomas early learned all he could about the Cherokee. Yonaguska, a foremost peace chief, or counselor, adopted Will Usdi as his son and encouraged his interest in Cherokee lore.

Thomas prospered as a trader, but the times were ominous for the Indians. Government efforts to remove them to present day Oklahoma culminated in the great exodus of 1838. Over seventeen thousand—from infant to aged—were gathered into stockades and moved westward in several groups. This trek became known as the Trail of Tears because so many suffered and died.

The Cherokee people lived and farmed in the mountains before you. Soldiers searched out their homes and led them away.

When two soldiers came for Tsali (Charlie) and his family, he left reluctantly but peacefully accompanied by his wife, two sons, and son-in-law.

The trip was long and wearying. Tsali's wife faltered. A soldier prodded her with his bayonet. It was a final, unbearable insult. Tsali disguised his anger and spoke calmly to his kinsmen in Cherokee. ''When we reach the turn in the trail, I will trip and fall. I will hold my ankle in pain. The soldiers will come to me. Leap on them. Take their guns. We will escape.''

CHESTNUT OAK

Tsali's plan worked too well. He stumbled and fell, and cried out as he grasped his ankle. A startled soldier came unsuspectingly to investigate. Tsali grabbed and jerked his feet from under him. The soldier fell back. His rifle fired. The bullet struck him dead. Meanwhile Tsali's kinsmen disarmed the other soldier who broke free and escaped.

RED OAK

Tsali knew that soldiers, many soldiers, would scour the mountains until they found him. It is better to die than give up. He led his family to a cave below the far side of the ridge you know as Thomas Divide.

Tsali was not aware of it, but more than a thousand

Cherokee had fled into the refuge of the Smoky Mountains and were surviving as best they could.

Meanwhile, detachments of Cherokee continued moving westward through the summer and into the following spring. Thousands died.

General Winfield Scott, the officer in charge, was a soldier who followed orders. This was a business he wished to complete and be done with. What to do about the widespread fugitives holed up in the mountains? It would take thousands of troops and many months to bring in the wary survivors.

The general knew of Tsali's escape and the death of the soldier. He summoned Will Thomas and gave his terms. Bring Tsali and his kinsmen to me. If they surrender and pay the penalty for the death of the soldier, I will recommend that the Indians still in the mountains be permitted to remain.

Will Thomas went alone. "The Cherokee are my friends. No harm will come to me." He searched out secret hideaways for two days until he came to the cave where Tsali dwelled. Tsali somberly heard the terms. "What will happen to my sons?" "I do not know." They faced each other in silence that brought no answers. He replied simply, "I will come."

The military acted swiftly. Tsali, his son-in-law, and oldest son were sentenced to be executed. They were granted a last wish: "If we must die, let it be by our own people. No blindfolds." Three Cherokee at the stockade were handed rifles. The last seconds ebbed numbly. A volley sounded and three figures sagged within the ropes that bound them.

The military kept its promise and the remaining Cherokee, including Tsali's wife and their youngest son, were permitted to stay. But they were not citizens and could not, therefore, own the land they lived on.

Will Thomas accepted the wish of a dying Yonaguska and became their chief. As a citizen, he could buy and own land. He accepted money due the Cherokee from the government and purchased land in his own name to be held in trust until possession by the Cherokee would be legally acknowledged. These are the lands of the Qualla Reservation.

TIMBER RATTLESNAKE

The **Rattlesnake Mountain Tunnel** is 415 feet long. *465.6 miles.*

The **Sherrill Cove Tunnel**, the last (or first) tunnel of the Blue Ridge Parkway, is 590 feet long. *466.3 miles.*

Ballhoot Scar
467.4 miles
elev. 2,550

The steep slashes down the face of the foreground ridge mark the shortcut whereby timber moved from forest to sawmill. "Ballhoot," came the strident cry of warning, and a ballhoot of logs plunged down the mountain, piling up in dust and jumble at the foot.

Raven Fork
467.9 miles
elev. 2,400

In the years immediately after the Revolution the Indian maintained a harassing type warfare against the advancing whites. Most of the violence occurred across the border in Tennessee.

According to local tradition a Cherokee warrior, the Raven, led a war party from his home on nearby Raven Fork into Tennessee. The foray was successful and they acquired several scalps. A vengeful party of whites trailed the Indians and came upon them during the height of their victory dance. In a sharp, brief conflict they killed the Raven and several of his followers.

Raven Fork enters the Oconaluftee a mile downstream. The shallow, graveled river bed was used as a crossing known as Ravensford.

View of Oconaluftee River Valley
468.4 miles
elev. 2,200

A Cherokee village named *E-gwan-ul-ti*, "by the river," stood a few miles downstream. The white man's pronunciation gave birth to Oconaluftee. The river drains the high valleys of the Eastern Smokies wilderness into the Tuckaseigee.

Oconaluftee River Bridge
469 miles
elev. 2,000

The bridge crossing the river enters U.S. 441 and Great Smoky Mountains National Park. The park was established in 1934, preserving an extensive area of primal forest. Many of the high peaks exceed 6,000 feet, and like the Black Mountains are covered with red spruce and Fraser fir.

Pioneer families settled in the fertile coves. The Pioneer Homestead, a short distance into the park, includes an exhibit of farm houses, barns, and a mill.

This region was also the ancestral home of the Cherokee. The town of Cherokee is a short distance left on U.S. 441. Here the drama *Unto These Hills* is presented each summer at the Mountainside Theater. The story relates the Indians' struggle to survive and remain in their homeland.

A Note about the Author:
Park Ranger and Naturalist, 1948–55

Bill Lord came to the Blue Ridge Parkway in 1948, a recently discharged infantryman and a still more recent graduate in zoology from Michigan State University. He was pursuing an ambition engendered in his Huck Finn and Tom Sawyer years to become a naturalist in the National Park Service. The Parkway didn't fit his concept of a national park. No grizzly bears or buffalo. But this was his chance to get into the service and he took it.

He found himself park rangering forty miles of the "scenic," not on a horse, but in a Pontiac coupe. He dwelled, not in a rustic cabin, but in a quiet upstairs apartment in the unhurried county seat of Floyd, Virginia, respectfully referred to by the local gentry as Floyd Court House.

He still remembers one crisp and sun-bright February morn. He had not yet been assigned a vehicle nor traveled the full length of his patrol. His time was spent in the Rocky Knob District Office learning the outline of his duties. The previous days had been cloudy and hemmed in, but now the sky was clear and the mountains revealed themselves. Warden Guy Dillon came in from a patrol in his pick-up truck and gestured to Bill. "Come along with me." Guy was mostly quiet the mile or two until they reached an overlook on Rocky Knob. He grinned and pointed over the mountain edge. "Go have a look." Guy knew that Bill would be wondrous at the view, and no one was ever more right. He felt aloft and weightless — right by the precipice, absorbing the shadowed, shaggy length of Rock Castle Gorge below and the singing, sweeping far-beyond of foothills, farm, and forest. That's where the guidebook was born:

> To tell the story
> True to the people and the land
> This main regard
> And be a chronicler
> A minstrel
> A worthy bard